THINKING SKILLS
a guide to logic and comprehension

by Richard W. Samson

introduction by Dr. Albert Upton

1975   Stamford, Connecticut   Innovative Sciences, Inc.

Some of the illustrations were originally drawn for *Creative Analysis* by Rex John Irvine; the rest are by the author.

Copyright © 1965 by Richard W. Samson. All rights reserved. Printed in the U.S.A.
Preface Copyright © 1975, 1981 by Innovative Sciences, Inc.
All rights reserved. No part of this book may be reproduced or utilized in any form or by any means, electronic or mechanical, including photocopying, recording or by any information storage and retrieval system, without permission in writing from the publisher. Inquiries should be addressed to Innovative Sciences, Inc., 300 Broad Street, Park Square Station, P.O. Box 15129, Stamford, CT 06901.

Library of Congress Catalog Card Number: 65-19951

ISBN 0-913804-10-X

To my wife

by Richard W. Samson

CREATIVE ANALYSIS (with Albert Upton)
THE MIND BUILDER
THE LANGUAGE LADDER
PROBLEM SOLVING IMPROVEMENT

Preface

More than a decade ago, in the first chapter of a book entitled THE MIND BUILDER, an age-old question was again raised: Can the mind be improved? The author set about to answer the question in the affirmative, first by citing supportive statistical evidence and then by describing the actual means to that end. The evidence was a more than 10-point IQ increase in one school year by a class of 256 college freshmen at Whittier College. The means, if it can be stated succintly, was this: when a person brings to the conscious level of awareness his own innate, intuitive reasoning processes, and then consciously practices the use of those processes over a period of time, he can improve the functional use of his mind. Within a few pages in this, the new edition of that book, you will come upon an explanation of these processes, now being called the "thinking skills." You will discover how language is at once the tool and the product; how words make it possible for us to think, and how thinking helps us create words. Perhaps you'll agree with many of the more than 16,000 previous readers that these are indeed profound ideas. But before you begin, it may be worthwhile to explore the background of how these ideas were developed over more than a generation into the "thinking skills."

We begin with the man whose ideas are the genesis of the concept of thinking skills, Dr. Albert Upton, the former professor of this book's author, later his colleague, and subsequently a close personal friend.

Dr. Eugene Brunelle, the founding editor of the JOURNAL OF CREATIVE BEHAVIOR, has called Upton "the finest mind I've ever run into in the academic world, [the man] that changed the course of my own intellectual interests." Upton was born in Denver, Colorado in 1897. He received his Ph D from the University of California at Berkeley in Philology and Literature in 1928. He taught at the universities of California, New Mexico, and Southern California, and spent more than 30 years at Whittier College as professor and Chairman of General Studies before retiring in 1966. It was during his tenure at Whittier that the ideas which have evolved into the concept of thinking skills were both spawned and developed.

PREFACE

Upton was early influenced by the work of C.K. Ogden and Ivor A. Richards. According to Upton, it was their epoch-making introduction to semantics, THE MEANING OF MEANING published in 1923, which set him to thinking.

Upton has written only one book. It was begun in 1933, but went through seven revisions over 30 years. It was not published outside of Whittier College until 1961. It is entitled DESIGN FOR THINKING.

Justice to this work cannot even be attempted here. But two key passages should be examined, for they reveal the author's insight. In the fourth chapter, "Meaning," he writes:

> *"If you would carve an axe handle, says the Chinese proverb, the model is in your hand. Now language is a tool of the brain, and it is the shape of that miraculous organ that will yield us the soundest principles of procedure."*

Now watch Upton's mind go to work on something at once so obvious, and yet so little understood—how we become conscious of things.

> *"... to be conscious of a finite thing (a thing with known boundaries), we must have at least two other things: a boundary and another infinite or indefinite thing, whose boundaries may be either partially known or unknowable except where they bound the finite thing.*
>
> *What do we mean when we say that boundaries and relations are things? Are not the water's edge and the land's end one and the same? Is the shoreline a part of the land or of the sea, or is it a line in its own right? It is easy to see that you cannot have a shoreline without a sea, a little harder to see that you cannot have a sea without a shore, and downright difficult for most of us to see that you can't have either without a shoreline. A person must draw that line somewhere. Wherever there is a sea, somebody must say to the water, so far you go and no farther; and to the land he must say, this is the end of you. And the relation between the one and the other is the act of delineation that went on in his head."*

PREFACE

The book was begun, according to Upton, as a "rallying point" for a curriculum experiment at Whittier. Upton's immediate concern was for developing his students' intellectual awareness, and he therefore set about to change the orientation of his classes. Instead of the traditional freshman English composition curriculum, he subjected his students to a rigorous process of taking apart and analyzing language. Upton encouraged his students to look at language as both a product and a tool.

Early in the development of The Experiment, Upton came to the conclusion that his students' learning would be enhanced by his absence from the classroom. He observed that his own intense questioning often intimidated students. "Nothing turns off a student faster than continually asking him what he means by what he says," he admitted. Upton broke his classes up into small groups for interactive discussion, each group being led by what he called a coach. Coaches were generally upper level students who showed a superior ability to both lead discussions and ask questions. He also developed "super coaches" to coach the coaches.

Upton's laboratory was the printed word, and not necessarily just those of poets and novelists. He delved into writings in the various sciences, even engineering. Upton found fodder for his developing intellectual system from writers as diverse as economic historian Charles Beard, and physicists Robert Oppenheimer and Albert Einstein. But possibly one of his most dramatic insights came from a life experience.

It is said that Archimedes discovered the principle of displacement by sitting in a bathtub; that Newton's insight into gravitational relationships struck him when an apple fell on his head; that Einstein first became concerned about the influence of space by noticing the independent movement of the compass needle at age five. For Upton it was the smell of formaldehyde.

Shortly after Upton became Chairman of General Studies at Whittier, his new administrative responsibilities caused him to examine the learning strategies of the various disciplines within the college.

PREFACE

As the story goes, he went down to the biology labs in the basement of the building in which his office was located. He soon perceived that biology set about to comprehend life by doing three sorts of analysis: taxonomy, anatomy and physiology. Sometime later, the smell of formaldehyde wafting up to his office triggered a profound insight. He said to himself, "If the biologist comes to know life through these three processes, then it must be true that the human mind analyzes all things through those processes." He chose synonyms for each of these analytical processes. Upton broadened taxonomy to classification; for anatomy, Upton used structure analysis; and for physiology came operation analysis. At once the three analytical "thinking skills" came into the Upton method.

The process of subjecting his ideas not simply to himself but to each new college generation provided the continual testing, retesting and development of his ideas. It also helped change the thinking of the students themselves. One student in particular played a key role in the future development of Upton's methods.

In 1952, native Californian Richard Samson decided to drop out of Stanford University at the end of his sophomore year. He had been a straight "A" student as a freshman, but in his second year he became disillusioned and uncertain of his own interests. After working for a few years, Samson decided to continue his undergraduate work but this time at the college in his hometown. He enrolled at Whittier in 1958 as a junior and decided to take one of Upton's courses.

He was immediately intrigued. Within a short time Samson became a coach and later a super coach in Upton's experiment. It occurred to Samson that Upton could improve his teaching effectiveness if students could be put through intellectual exercises along the lines of the various analytical processes. With Upton's encouragement Samson went to work. James Romig, a classmate who later taught Upton's courses upon the latter's retirement, said that Samson "had an incredible genius for developing intellectual puzzles." Samson's exercises eventually became the "Graded Exercises in Analysis." To the exercises was added a text written by Samson under Upton's close supervision.

The Whittier Experiment perhaps would have been nothing more that just a Whittier experiment if a different kind of experiment hadn't been made. With the boost that the Upton courses re-

PREFACE

ceived with Samson's graded exercises, Dr. Roberta Foresberg of Whittier was struck by the probability that students who went through the Graded Exercises would in fact show measurable IQ gains. In 1959, entering freshmen at Whittier were given a standardized IQ test. They then went through the "Basic Communications" course, the "Graded Exercises in Analysis." In May 1960, they were retested. The students showed on the mean more than a 10-point increase. Every student went up. The smallest increase was 6 points; the largest was 32. Samson urged the college to send out a news release on the results. Later he checked the mailing list, and suggested that the New York TIMES be added to the list.

The release was received at the Times by education editor Fred Hechinger. He thought it interesting enough to interview Upton about it. On June 27th, 1960 the TIMES carried a front-page article under the headline "Student IQ's Rise in California Test." Hechinger wrote: "Evidence that applied human intelligence can be dramatically increased has been offered by an experiment conducted by a California professor after twenty-five years of research. The results of the test, administered at Whittier College, may offer the key to the release of native but unused brain power in the majority of persons."

"The Upton Method," Hechinger continued, "aims at the expansion of the human capacity to see an analogy between an idea, a word or a metaphor he knows and an idea he wants to understand. Once the student understands this, he has learned how his tools of thought work."

Then he quoted Upton. "'We don't know whether native intelligence may be increased, because we don't know what it is. But we can train people to solve problems they could not solve before.'"

To an IQ-conscious nation, this was incredible. The article was syndicated and editorialized upon throughout the country and picked up by the world press. Upton's experiment literally shocked a nation which had been led to believe that IQ's were fixed and immutable.

Within the next three years things happened swiftly. The course-work called "Graded Exercises in Analysis" was published with the title CREATIVE ANALYSIS by a press set up at Whittier College. Two years later it was republished by E. P. Dutton with the same title.

PREFACE

Upton accepted an invitation to speak to the Chairman of Finance for the Ford Motor Company. The result was that Ford decided to underwrite the publishing of Upton's DESIGN FOR THINKING. In 1961, Stanford University Press put it in print. The Whittier Experiment was the subject of high-level discussion throughout the country. One of this country's most eminent cognitive psychologists, J. P. Guilford, author of IQ tests and developer of the "Structure of Intellect" theory, read CREATIVE ANALYSIS. He recommended it by name in his NATURE OF HUMAN INTELLIGENCE published by McGraw-Hill in 1967.

Samson was graduated from Whittier in 1960 but decided to stay on as a research assistant with Upton to help further translate the Upton methods into more easily understood concepts. The result was a book for the lay public, published by E. P. Dutton in 1965 under the title THE MIND BUILDER.

One of its readers was Charles F. Adams, founder of Innovative Sciences, Inc. Adams, who was deeply committed to improving the learning process by developing new learning strategies, saw in THE MIND BUILDER a methodology for improving the teaching of all academic content. In 1971, with ISI just off the drawing boards, Adams decided to attempt to turn Upton's methods into a learning technology. He called Samson together with his newly organized design staff. Within less than a year Samson had helped ISI fashion the Upton methods into what is now the most critical component in ISI's learning system, "Logic and Comprehension."

In 1972, ISI introduced a language-reading program called Think and a mathematics program called Intuitive Math to the public schools, first on the East Coast, and then across the United States. By late 1975, more than 900 school systems and upwards of 4,000 teachers had been exposed to this adaptation of Upton's methods.

Students from 5th grade to 12th grade have thus been exposed to thinking skills in reading, language and mathematics. The results have startled educators. Dr. Oren Glick, program evaluator for Franklin Pierce School District in Tacoma, Washington, reported that junior and senior high students using Think and Intuitive Math in three separate schools showed increased aptitude scores, improved attitudes toward English and math, and enhanced self-concept of ability.

PREFACE

Seventh graders in a Detroit inner city school using Think made the highest reading gains they had ever recorded. They even improved their daily attendance record.

A teacher in Newman, California, reported that Think "actually motivated non-achievers into pursuit of knowledge—even on *their own* time!" (her emphasis).

The evidence is abundant and clear, and teachers are reporting it from every learning setting imaginable. When you expose learners to their own thinking skills within their academic subject-matter classes, they not only learn faster and better, they also feel better about themselves.

Teachers exposed to this technology have thirsted for more. To fill that need, Innovative Sciences decided to republish THE MIND BUILDER and recast its title more closely to the role it plays with teachers and interested educators.

To many, a cognitive revolution is underway but it is still in its formative stages. They wonder what the future will be like when a significant portion of the population has gained mastery over the traditional intuitive functions of thought. How much more sensitively and creatively will people act and interact? How will life be different?

In the meantime you are invited to join the revolution. This book introduces to the general public the key elements of Upton's Method. The exercises will lift your thinking ability to the mental plateau which is achieved by a more enlightened use of words. As you progress through the exercises you will find yourself not only thinking, but thinking about how to think. Your intuitive mental processes will be marshaled for conscious inspection and direction. You will be using your brain more consistently in the reflective mode that is man's unique gift.

If you are a member of the teaching profession, think of this book not merely as food for your students' growth, but as food for a kind of metamorphosis. Be conscious of helping them gain a new kind of functioning, not a mere brightening of what they already have. As Thoreau said, "There is more day to dawn, the sun is but a morning star."

E. GENE MARR –NOVEMBER 1975
INNOVATIVE SCIENCES, INC.

PREFACE TO THE 1981 EDITION

In the original Preface to this book, it is noted that "...a cognitive revolution is underway, but it is still in its formative stages." Six years later, I am pleased to report that this "revolution" has matured into a full-fledged, powerful, world-wide movment. The *thinking skills* theory and methods of Dr. Albert Upton and Richard Samson, detailed so clearly in THINKING SKILLS, have played a significant role in the growth of this movement.

All around the world, educators now recognize as imperative the need to teach students to think — to develop and maximize the cognitive processes or *thinking skills* which are the mental muscles of the mind. A quick glance through any of the noted educational journals such as *Educational Leadership, Phi Delta Kappan, The Gifted Child Quarterly, The Reading Teacher,* etc. reveals article after article citing the urgent need for thinking skills instruction in our classrooms.

Even many of those who, in the seventies, led the 'return to basics' have discovered that the "three r's" alone are not sufficient goals for education — that students must be taught to think, as well. Time and again researchers report that students who have mastered the 'basics' do not necessarily have any comprehension of what they have learned. Nor are they capable of thinking with and applying what they have learned to solve even simple real-life problems. A commonly voiced conclusion is that of the Fall, 1979 report of the National Assessment of Education Progress: "...narrowing the curriculum in response to the back-to-basics movement has resulted in insufficient attention to higher-level processes, including problem-solving." The value of such learning is being increasingly questioned.

Consistently, and with increasing urgency, educators identify the development of students' thinking skills and problem-solving abilities as the first priority of education in the eighties. Consequently, there is an obvious need for workable strategies to aid in the fulfillment of this priority, and the demand for copies of this text has steadily increased. THINKING SKILLS provides for teachers, students and the interested public a tested, proven system for improving thinking ability. As such, it can serve as the natural core of any personal or group thinking development effort. Results over the years consistently prove its power.

After reading and working through THINKING SKILLS, perhaps you will agree with thousands of previous readers — thinking skills instruction represents the most logical interpretation of 'back-to-basics.'

JOHN GLADE - JANUARY, 1981
Innovative Sciences, THINK, Inc.

Contents

PREFACE v
INTRODUCTION xv
   1. What Is "Thinking"? 17
   2. The Role of Words in Thing-Making 27
   3. The Role of Words in Qualification 35
   4. The Role of Words in Classification 40
   5. The Role of Words in Structure Analysis 45
   6. The Role of Words in Operation Analysis 50
   7. The Role of Words in Analogy 57
   8. Ambiguity: Some Words Have Many Meanings 60
   9. How Words Change Their Meanings 63
 10. Progressive Ambiguity Helps the Growth of Knowledge ... 70
 11. Toward a New Mental Plateau? 79

EXERCISES 81
   Directions 83
   Level 1—Very Easy 84
   Level 2—Easy 91
   Level 3—Easy-Medium 101
   Level 4—Medium 115
   Level 5—Medium-Difficult 133
   Level 6—Difficult 151
   Level 7—Very Difficult 167
ANSWERS TO EXERCISES 183

Introduction

This is a book about the art of making sense. The focus is **on** language as the means.

In the beginning were grunts and squeals and they voiced, without forethought, the pleasures and pains of the beasts that made them. Then man, the inventor, built of them a machine he called language (after his own tongue); but the machine grew and overwhelmed its maker. Like fire and water it became both good servant and bad master.

The citizen of contemporary civilization depends to an ever-increasing degree upon the instrument of language to make survival possible and bearable. With the complicated machines of science, modern man transforms the physical world in which he lives. But often the transformation leads to misery and madness, for he has yet to transform the kingdom within himself. Change for the better demands a redesigning of our linguistic engine by the same processes of analysis, experiment, and rigorous training which have effected such radical alterations in our physical world.

Human ingenuity has not, and will not, fail us here; but the hour is late. A constructive science of language (for language is the vehicle of reason) can save us from the destructive technologies of mechanization. This book presents the first principles of such a science. It surveys in systematic manner the ways in which words work, on the assumption that a working knowledge of any mechanism is a vital step in the direction of its efficient use.

But, if we would add wisdom to our knowledge, we must learn by doing. This book is addressed to those who are willing to work — to those whose minds are on the march. The rewards are worthy of the effort.

Language is a mirror in which man gazes upon himself; but it is a magic mirror with the power to change itself and the being it reflects. A lively awareness of this fact may enable the clear-sighted to make his language into a master instrument of self-discipline and hence of self-emancipation.

ALBERT UPTON
Whittier, California

CHAPTER 1

What Is "Thinking"?

If we are to improve our thinking, we must first understand what thinking is. According to Professor Upton's "system," thinking (or the functioning mind) may be divided into seven basic phases:

1. WORDS: We let words (together with numbers and other symbols) mean things.
2. THING-MAKING: We make mental pictures of things when we interpret sensations.
3. QUALIFICATIONS: We notice the qualities of things: how things are alike and how they differ.
4. CLASSIFICATION: We mentally sort things into classes, types, or families.
5. STRUCTURE ANALYSIS: We observe how things are made: break structural wholes into component parts.
6. OPERATION ANALYSIS: We notice how things happen: in what successive stages.
7. ANALOGY: We see how seemingly unconnected situations are alike, forming parallel relations in different "worlds of thought."

Let us examine briefly each of these seven phases of thought.

WORDS

Our minds give words to things: *ring* to a band worn on the finger, or the sound of a bell; *hand* to the extremity of a man's arm, or a number of playing cards; *set* to a collection of something, the act of positioning an object, or the healing process of a broken bone.

Yet words are more than vehicles of communication; they are also tools of thought. We manipulate our thoughts by manipulating words. By shifting and patterning words such as *airplane, snow,* and *skis,* a man may imagine an airplane with skis — a new invention.

This verbal nature of thought permeates and facilitates all the thinking we do, whether thing-making, qualification, classification, structure analysis, operation analysis, or analogy. In qualification, for example, the words *red, cold,* and *fast* may help us to abstract color from an apple, temperature from a winter day, and velocity from a moving train. Without verbal tools, we probably could not think. We need words to symbolize things, qualities, classes, parts, wholes, happenings, stages, and abstract relations. The use of language, elevating man from the apes, facilitates and perhaps makes possible conscious thought in all its higher forms.

Working through the other six phases of thought, words cut our world of experience into comprehensible segments — into word "bits" that make thoughts. God himself, Genesis might lead us to believe, used words to slice the boundless universe he was creating into regions he could keep track of: "God divided the light from the darkness. And God called the light Day, and the darkness he called Night." In a sense, we too divide the light from the darkness whenever we utter the words *day* and *night.* With other words, God carved out the realms of the world we now live on: "And God said, 'Let the waters under the heaven be gathered together unto one place, and let the dry land appear' . . . And God called the dry land Earth; and the gathering together of the waters called he Seas . . ." With words, we too "gather the waters unto one place" and "let the dry land appear" — in our minds. In *Design for Thinking,* Albert Upton says, "Whenever there is a sea, somebody must say to the water, so far you go and no farther; and to the land he must say, this is the end of you. And the relation between the one and the other is the act of delineation that went on in his head." This "act of delineation" is a symbolic one. With words or some other type of symbol in his mind, "a person must draw that line somewhere." There are no lines, no distinctions, until we create them with some type of symbol; and words are our most intimate symbols.

In a sense, each of us is god of the world within his head. We can divide, delineate, or distinguish whatever we wish — but only in proportion to our verbal skill. For words help us to create the mind's universe: "gather unto one place" the waters of experience and "let appear" the lands of meaning.

Chapters 3 through 8 discuss the role of words in each of the other six phases of thought. The balance of this chapter will give brief definitions of these six phases.

THING-MAKING

Our minds "make" objects out of sensations. Different patterns of light are interpreted as a tree, as an automobile, or as the man in the moon. Different patterns of sound are experienced as thunder, as a car screeching to a halt, or as a symphony.

You may say, "But the mind doesn't *make* things; it simply becomes *aware* of things." Does it? On a chart to test for color-blindness, a series of red dots may be arranged among green, blue, and yellow dots to make out the number 2. Is the 2 "really there"? The "thing" that is seen depends on the person. For a normal person there is a 2; for a color-blind man, simply meaningless dots. Since different people see different things, might we not call into question the "real" existence of the 2, apart from human consciousness? We must, of course, assume that *something* is there, something to reflect light to our eyes so that we may see a 2 or simply dots. But who is to say what that "real something," apart from human consciousness, is? The important thing for us to realize is that our own minds help shape what we see, help "make things" out of the raw sensory data which come streaming in through our eyes, ears, nose, mouth, and fingertips.

The world simply gives us light waves, sound waves, chemical reactions, and other stimuli which our sense organs can accept and send to the brain. The mind may then do something with these sensations. Often, sensations may be ignored. Though sound waves from a conversation reach your ears and your brain, you may not hear what is said if you are reading.

Sensations may be interpreted in different ways under different circumstances. If you are hungry, you may see an apple as a juicy, sweet thing; if you want to use an apple as part of a centerpiece, you may see it as a red, round, lovely thing; if you are angry at someone, you may see an apple as a projectile. The light waves are interpreted in different ways, so that different aspects of the apple stand out. This selective emphasis of perception is true of all that we experience.

Because we are human beings with sense organs and brains, certain stimuli take on particular meanings for us. Light waves, sound waves, pressures, and chemical reactions (interpreted this way or that) become "things" in our minds. Photons striking our retinas become the Statue of Liberty in the distance. Air molecules vibrating in a certain pattern become a child's cry for help.

Qualification

Our minds separate qualities from things: "red" from a rose, "small" from a pin, "interesting" from a book, "democratic" from a government.

Qualification is the opposite of thing-making. You hear a rumbling noise. Is it thunder? Looking into the sky, you see nothing at first; then you make out a jet airplane. This is thing-making — the interpretation of sensory data, *making* something of sights and sounds. Once you have made an airplane of the sound and light, you may describe it. You may say, "It is shiny" or "It is fast." This is qualification: describing something.

When you describe or qualify objects, you notice their aspects, not their parts: the greenness, not the branch, of a tree; the fragrance, not the blossom, of a flower; the flexibility, not the trunk, of an elephant; the friendliness, not the suburbs, of a city. Qualities are not things you can touch or handle. Yet, though they are more elusive than wind or shadows, they are the basic ingredients of all substantial bodies. A banana is made of "yellow," "oblong," and "sweet." A New York apartment building is made of "tall," "urban," and "inhabited."

A thing is no more than the layered qualities which make it up. Were it not for these qualities, we could not know what a thing is. We could not tell it from anything else. Let us consider an orange and a lemon. How do we tell them apart? They are made of different qualities. The orange is made of sweetness, orangeness, and roundness. The lemon is made of sourness, yellowness, and ovalness. If we were to subtract the sweetness from the orange and the sourness from the lemon, we would become less able to distinguish them, though we could still tell them apart by their color and shape. If we were to take away the orangeness from the orange and the yellowness from the lemon, we would become still less able to tell the two things apart. But there would still remain some distinguishing qualities. By observing the differing shapes we could tell the two tasteless and colorless objects apart. If we were to take away the roundness and the ovalness of all other qualities of the objects, we could not tell them apart at all. In fact, they would not exist, in our minds. A solid object is a combination of ethereal qualities, ghosts which enable us to know what the thing is, how it differs from other quality-combinations, other things.

When you qualify, you divide an object into "parts" which are not really parts at all in the physical sense. You divide a rosebush into its color, shape, size, and fragrance, not into its petals, stems, roots, and atoms. The result of this abstracting process is that you can tell how things are similar to and different from other things. This knowledge of similarities and differences enables you to classify, to arrange your thoughts into meaningful patterns.

Classification

Our minds separate classes into sub-classes: human beings into adults and children; nations into allies, neutrals, and enemies; writing implements into pens, pencils, crayons, and chalk. Classification is simply the sorting of things into groups according to some purpose.

When you speak of *types* of things as opposed to *parts* of things or *stages* of things, you are classifying. When you analyze the map of the United States, naming the states and saying how they fit together, you are performing a structure analysis, dividing a static thing into its spatial elements. This is not classification. When you say that a year has twelve months, starting with January, continuing with February and ending with December; that January has thirty-one days; that a day has twenty-four hours; that an hour has sixty minutes; and that a minute has sixty seconds, you are not classifying. You are performing an operation analysis: you are saying how something that happens is divided into time-elements — into stages and sub-stages.

But if you say that a human being is an animal, that human beings are either male or female, that males are either men or boys, and that boys are either big or little, you are classifying. You are placing things into mental groups according to their similarities and differences. Classification has to do with types, sorts, classes. Roses are sorts of bushes, bushes are sorts of plants; clocks are sorts of timepieces, timepieces are sorts of measuring instruments; sergeants are sorts of soldiers, soldiers are sorts of servicemen. Similar things are put into the same group; different things are put into different groups. The key to classification is qualification — the observation of similarities and differences, which results in the systematic sorting of things into classes.

Classification may be expressed in diagrammatic form, as follows.

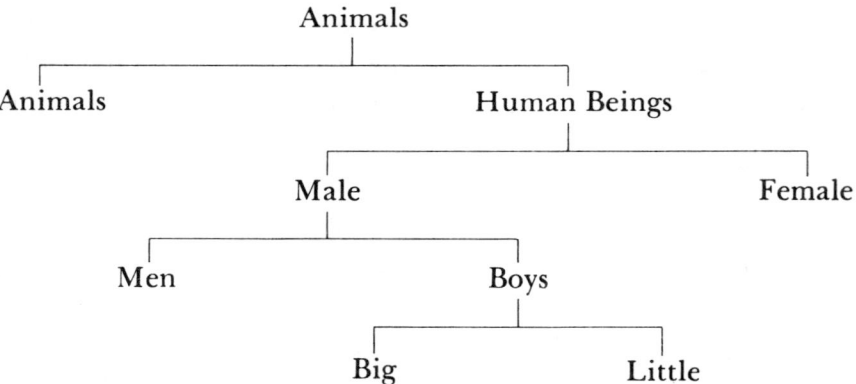

Structure Analysis

Our minds divide wholes into parts: a man's body into head, trunk, and limbs; a chair into seat, back, and legs; the Earth into atmosphere, crust, and core.

There are many types of thoughts we can think about things.

Not all of them are structural thoughts. How do we tell the difference? Let us consider eggs. When the most famous of all eggs, Humpty Dumpty, fell from the wall, the unhappy result was of a structural nature: pieces, parts — spatial elements of a static whole.

If, instead of "breaking" an egg into parts, you take a basket containing many different kinds of eggs and "break them down" into types (chicken eggs, duck eggs, pigeon eggs), you are classifying, not analyzing, the physical parts of a structure. If you take an egg and "break it down" into the things which happen to it (a hen lays it, a baby chick grows inside it, the chick pecks through its shell and is born from it), you are analyzing an operation, not a static structure; you are "breaking" something into "time-parts" rather than physical parts in a purely spatial sense. If you take an egg and "break it down" into its attributes (white, ovular, edible, fragile), you are qualifying it, not analyzing its structure — the spatial arrangement of its parts.

Structure analysis is the process of dividing something thought of as static (a physical whole) into spatial parts: a tree into roots, trunk, limbs, and leaves; a knife into handle and blade; the Bible into books, chapters, pages, and verses. Even a baseball game (a rapidly changing event) can be subjected to structure analysis; "frozen" at a point in time, it may be divided into structural parts such as the field, the pitcher, the catcher, the first baseman, the bat, the ball, the umpire, an outfielder's mitt. Structure analysis is the division of anything thought of as filling space (but not time) into subordinate spatial elements.

There is, of course, a right way and a wrong way to go about structure analysis. This is the lesson to be drawn from Humpty Dumpty's shattering experience. The parts into which that imprudent egg divided himself were of little use to anyone. Here is a more useful way to "break" an egg into parts:

$$\text{Egg} \begin{cases} \text{Shell} \\ \text{"Insides"} \begin{cases} \text{Yolk} \\ \text{White} \\ \text{Membrane} \end{cases} \end{cases}$$

Operation Analysis

Our minds divide happenings into stages: a day into morning, afternoon, and night; a play into Act I, Act II, and Act III; history into ancient times, the Middle Ages, the Renaissance, and modern times.

In operation analysis, the sort of dividing we do has to do with successive points in time. After his fall, Humpty Dumpty was divided into parts, not stages; the points of division (cracks) were in space, not time. A shattered egg is a structure, not an operation. But a *shattering* egg is an operation and can thus be divided into stages: slipping from the wall, falling through the air, hitting the ground, and shattering to bits. Each stage is divided from the next at some point in time. At 1:00 P.M. Humpty Dumpty begins to totter; at 1:03 he slips from the wall and starts his fall; under the grip of gravity, he tumbles end over end, until at 1:04 he makes contact with the ground; the shattering stage continues for a minute, until at 1:05 all the pieces lie still, awaiting the historic inability of the king's horses and men. Successive "times" artificially separate the total event into arbitrary stretches during which certain types of change take place.

An operation may be described as a changing structure. Operation analysis, then, tells how a structure changes. Structure analysis is the division of a thing into spatial elements at a *fixed* point in time — that is, when change does not occur or is ignored. Operation analysis is what we do when we keep track of how structures change. The United States, now, is a structure which may be divided into fifty parts. In 1778, the United States was a different structure which could be divided into thirteen parts. When we examine the changes between 1778 and now (the gradual acquisition of new states), we introduce the concept of alteration in time; we may think of the historical periods of the total period of national growth, how change took place; this is operation analysis.

The type of "inclusion" is the important distinction. Parts of structures extend over quantities of space; stages of operations extend over quantities of time. Venus is a part of the solar system; but Venus turning on its axis (a Venusian day) is a stage of Venus circling the sun (a Venusian year). Parts grasp spatial areas or contents; stages grasp temporal periods. The keys, strings, and pedals of a piano fill space; the verses and choruses of a song fill time. Operation analysis is the division of events into constituent periods of change.

Operation analysis may be represented graphically in "outline" form, thus:

    Life
       Birth
       Life
           Childhood
           Adolescence
           Adulthood
       Death

Analogy

Our minds see that the relation between two things is similar to the relation between two other things: that dawn is to nightfall as birth is to death; that a limb is to a tree as an arm is to a man; that a calf is to a cow as a child is to a woman; that the inmost self is to the body as a worshiper is to a temple.

Two things have a relation similar to the relation of two other things. A is to B as C is to D, or

$$\frac{A}{B} = \frac{C}{D}$$

Consider the analogy "shovel is to furnace as spoon is to mouth." A shovel (A) carries coal to a furnace (B) as a spoon (C) takes food to a mouth (D). The equals mark means that the two relations are similar. The relation "carries coal to" is similar to the relation "takes food to." The similarity between the relations might be expressed as follows: "transports fuel to." Both a shovel and a spoon transport fuel to a place where it will be consumed.

All analogies follow this pattern. Two things relate to each other in the same way that two other things relate to each other.

Analogies are unique in that they express similarity between relations, not direct similarity between things. You do not see an analogy when you see that the moon and a basketball are alike in shape; that similarity is directly between two things, not between two relations (involving a total of four things). But you see an analogy if you see that the moon is related to the Earth as Hungary is related to Russia; the similarity is between two relations: the "orbiting" relation of Earth's satellite is similar to the "dominating political influence" relation of Russia's satellite. Two relations come together into a larger common relation.

What is thinking? Essentially, it is a combination of seven phases: WORDS, THING-MAKING, QUALIFICATION, CLASSIFICATION, STRUCTURE ANALYSIS, OPERATION ANALYSIS, and ANALOGY.

The first phase, words, appears to control and guide all the other phases. Words (together with numbers and other such symbols of meaning) act as markers or signs to help us keep track of our mental explorations. Words enable us to symbolize things, qualities, types, parts, stages, and abstract relations. Words are tools of thought, whatever its pattern, helping us to analyze the world around us.

By improving your use of words as tools of analysis, you can improve your thinking. The exercises in this book are intended to help you do just that.

First, you may profit by examining the role of language in the thinking you do. How do words control and guide thing-making, qualification, classification, structure analysis, operation analysis, and analogy?

CHAPTER 2

The Role of Words in Thing-Making

Words influence what we see; they help us "make things" out of the raw data of sensation. The words *dipper* and *cross* help us make a "Big Dipper" and a "Southern Cross" out of stars which have no actual lines joining them. With words fashioning our perceptions, we see a man in the moon, animals in clouds, mountains in sand dunes. When Albert Upton looks at the picture of the moon on his office wall, he does not see craters; he sees "blisters." Because he has for so many years tried to get students to see "blisters," as an exercise in thing-making, he himself now finds it difficult to see craters. His mind interprets the circular shadings as projections rather than depressions; thus the "craters" bulge out. The word *blister* plays a role in this unusual perception.

The things we perceive do not pop into consciousness automatically. Before a sensory stimulus "becomes" an object, it must be patterned in someone's mind. "It's a bird. It's a plane. It's Superman!" The words *bird, plane,* and *Superman* facilitate the interpretation of pattern. Sailors often face the task of deciding what distant "somethings" are. Henry David Thoreau, in *Cape Cod,* writes that mariners sometimes run ashore, even though they "see" the land. A bank one hundred yards away may be "seen" as a mountain several miles away. Once when Thoreau was in an oyster boat at night, he almost ran aground because the "lighthouse" toward which he was steering turned out to be the light issuing from the cracks of a fisherman's house. Before we can recognize something, we must go through the process of interpreting what our senses tell us by *making something* of it.

Ordinarily, this process of thing-making happens so quickly that we do not realize what we are doing. We look across the room and see a chair. We usually do not notice that there is a split second between our first *sight* of the object and our *recognition* of it, a split second in which we see no more than unpatterned color and shade, and must scan our memory for similar impressions, finally "recognizing" the thing as a chair. Accompanying and encouraging this recognition of the thing itself is a sub-vocal utterance of a symbol: we think the word *chair* and see the chair at the same time.

In order to appreciate the role of words in thing-making, we must first realize that "things" exist not in the "outside world" but in the mind. In order for things to exist, we must interpret the unpatterned waves of sensation which come streaming in through our senses.

The fact that the mind creates "things" may be illustrated by a paradox. If a tree falls in a forest when no one is there, is there any sound?

We may as well begin with the realization that this paradox, like many others, involves an ambiguous word: *sound*. In one sense of the word, "sound" is noise, something we experience as part of our consciousness. In another sense of the word, "sound" is a physical (not a mental) thing — sound waves, patterns of condensation and rarefaction of air, a thing outside the mind, possessing no "loudness" (which is an experience requiring a mind in which to exist). If no one is in the forest when the tree falls, there can be no "sound" (noise) because there is no mind in which this experience of loudness can take place. But there is "sound" in the sense of physical sound waves, the hypothetical stimulus of loudness (provided, of course, that there is someone somewhere to hypothesize the waves). This paradox brings up the question, "What things exist 'out there' and what things exist only in our minds?"

If we are to understand how our minds "make things" out of the sensory stimuli which stream in through our eyes, ears, and fingertips, we must first of all draw a line between the things which belong to the mind only and the things which belong to the "external world" only.

How shall we draw the line? Loudness or noise, we have decided, belongs in the mind; sound waves, we say, belong to the "external world." What about an apple, a physical object that we can see and touch? If there is an apple on a table before you and you close your eyes, what is "really there"? Is the apple a red object, in reality? Isn't the apple's redness an experience which takes place in your mind, just as the crash of a falling tree takes place in your mind? You feel the apple and it is cold. Isn't this coldness an experience, something which requires a mind for existence? It is firm and round. Are not these things experiences, too? What, then, is the apple "out there"? It is, we may say, a cause of stimulation, just as sound waves are a cause of stimulation for the experience of loudness. As far as the mind is concerned, it is simply a hypothetical *something*, a cause of stimulation.

This, then, is the line we must draw. In the "outside world" there are no colors, no sounds (experiences of loudness, softness, shrillness, lowness), no feelings of cold, warm, or hot, no shapes, no patterns, no "heaviness," no joy, no sorrow. There are only causes of stimulation, hypothetical physical stimuli which produce experiences in minds: "air waves" which produce noises; "light waves" which produce colors and shapes; hypothetical atomic "somethings" which, when "touched," produce feelings of heat, cold, hardness, heaviness. The things of the external world are hypothetical stimuli; the things of the mind are experiences assumed to result from these stimuli — experiences of shape, texture, size, color, noise, emotion. There are no loud crashes or red apples in "reality." There are only stimuli which the mind converts or "makes into" loud crashes and red apples. If a tree falls in a forest when no one is there, not only is there no sound, there is no forest either. Crashes and trees are made by "fools like you and me" but only God can make their stimuli.

Thing-making is the process by which the raw data of the "real world" are made into the things of the mind. But to say that we make things in our minds is not to deny the existence of "real things, out there." The point is that we must not attribute to external "reality" things that only a mind can experience. If a camera makes a two-dimensional photograph of a landscape, it would be wrong to say that the landscape is two-dimensional, too. The camera's lens may distort the "reality" it focuses. A filter over the lens may alter the shading. The film may record only black and white, though the hills and valleys are green, yellow, and brown. We are mental cameras. The "pictures" we record bear a relation to the hypothetical reality outside; but these pictures are not the reality. They are new things created according to our structure, our sensory, emotional, and logical make-up. Equally, the "realities" outside are not the pictures (things) in our heads. We can never know precisely what these outside things are. We can only look at our internal photographs and guess at the nature of the forces which produced them. Though we may speculate about them, their actual nature must remain one of the mysteries of our existence. The important point to comprehend is that we take in the hypothetical light of sensation and then filter it and focus it in the mind's camera eye, transforming it into a picture, a "thing," something quite apart from the assumed source of its being.

This transformation of sensory stimuli into "things," or mental pictures, is aided by words. Animals, lacking the human capacity for speech, cannot see the same things that we see. Can a crow "see" the scarecrow which frightens it from a garden? Not really. If the crow could identify the scarecrow *as* a scarecrow, it would realize its harmlessness. What, then, does the crow see? We can only speculate. If the crow is conscious at all (possessing, perhaps, a rudimentary symbolic ability), it probably sees no more than a vague form, a "large, menacing thing." Without the symbolic tools necessary to analyze the object, the crow cannot tell it from a human being. In fact, to the crow there are probably no such things as "human beings."

Able to symbolize the sights and sounds around us, we are much more aware of things than crows. Yet, beyond the limits of our analytic development, we too lump dissimilar things together when we cannot find words to discriminate between them. Like the raven at the Catalina aviary we can only croak, "It's all the same, it's all the same."

A magician's trick will illustrate the point. The magician's female assistant, clad in a green bathing suit, climbs into the barrel of a cannon. The magician then suspends, by cables, a sealed chest several feet above the stage. Pointing the cannon toward the suspended chest, he lights the fuse. There is an explosion, but contrary to expectations the girl is not propelled from the cannon. The magician then lowers the chest and unseals it. To the amazement of the spectators, the girl emerges, smiling. How did she get from the cannon to the sealed, suspended chest?

The magician's trick was to place a *second* assistant, also clad in a green bathing suit, into the chest before the start of the act. A scarecrow or even a mannequin would not have fooled the audience. But another girl, though of slightly different weight, height, hair color, and facial expression, was sufficiently similar to transcend their powers of discrimination. Those in the audience who may have figured out the trick did so because they were skillful at manipulating symbols. They used words and private symbolic images in an internal conversation with themselves. They *saw more* than the others; they saw a *particular* girl, not just a generalized "girl in a green bathing suit."

Because of our symbolic limitations, many "scarecrows" fill our daily lives. Chances are that a man who speaks only of "wine" cannot taste Beaujolais (he can "taste" only "wine," for that is all he can distinguish). An increasingly discriminating vocabulary accompanies the developing connoisseur's ability to taste Graves, Chablis, and Sauterne. The inability to identify varieties of wine is like being able to see red, while being blind to vermilion, scarlet, and carmine.

We become increasingly aware of things as we develop increasingly discriminating vocabularies. In the Garden of Eden, Adam became aware of the different types of animals only as he found names for them. (Incidentally, did Adam "see" animals as mammals?)

As newborn children, all of us begin our mental lives with

little more than an awareness of "figure and ground," vague things against a background of space. The unfolding awareness of Mother, Teddy Bear, strangers, trees, and stars is paralleled by the development of a vocabulary to stand for such things. In order to *know*, we must learn to *say*.

One of the most impressive functions of words is their ability to let us see things relatively and from different levels of awareness. Words not only help us to impose patterns within our environment, but also to emphasize different aspects of similarly perceived objects. We do not see things "absolutely," but from one point of view or another, depending on the words we use. If we call a person a "woman," her feminine qualities stand out in our minds; if we call her a "gossip," her talkativeness comes forward, while other qualities recede. If we call a whale a "fish," we think of its tail and watery habitat; if we call it a "mammal," we think of its warm-bloodedness and suckling ability. We fashion things in our minds according to the names we give them, emphasizing now this quality, now that.

Words enable us to see things in many ways and on various levels of abstraction. When we look into the night sky and see the Big Dipper, the word *dipper* helps to create in our minds something which does not exist in "reality." There are no perceived physical connections between the stars which make it up. We ordinarily see the stars as more or less randomly placed in space. Our minds must find a pattern, symbolically "making" a dipper of the stars. (Incidentally, the word *astronomer* comes from two words meaning "star arranger" in Latin and Greek.)

Actually, there are no random stars until someone makes them into "random stars." Nor are there individual stars, until someone makes them in his mind, with the help of words. How can there be a "star" unless there is some way to identify one, to tell it from a moon or comet? Just as we create the Big Dipper by imposing a pattern on random stars, so we create an individual star by imposing a pattern on *it*. This "pattern" is what we might call its "definition," the criterion by which we tell it from other things. This pattern, given form by the word *star*, might go something like this: "bright object in the heavens which shines by its own light and is not a satellite of another celestial object." In order for there to be a star, as distinct from other objects, a complex mental process is necessary — the use of a word or other symbol to identify the object according to its qualities, mentally placing it with like objects and distinguishing it from unlike objects, thus determining what it "is."

A name is really the label of a "concept" or class of experiences. The word *star* identifies a class of experiences which are alike. We have learned that certain things are bright, small, and distant in the night sky, and we have been told that they shine by their own light like the sun; so we give them the same name. The name could be anything, as long as we use it consistently. English-speaking people have settled on the word *star*. Now this word serves as a kind of marker or reminder in our minds. When we use it, we are reminded of our experiences of various scattered pinpoints of light. Without such a label or tag, we would have no way of binding together these diverse experiences in our consciousness. We could not see the stars, just as we cannot see the Big Dipper if we have no name to tell us what to look for.

Can a child see a star if he does not know what the word means and has no private symbol of his own? No doubt he can see a "bright object in the sky," but he cannot see it *as a star* if he has no label to classify it with like things and distinguish it from unlike things. If he cannot distinguish a star from Mars or Venus, he cannot see a star *as* a star, that is to say, he cannot "tell" it from a planet.

This intimate relation between words and things is true of all that we experience. What a thing is for us depends upon the words we use to identify it.

Words cannot, of course, create things which "aren't there." If you call an alligator an apple, it will not become red, round, and luscious, no matter how much you polish it. "If you call a tail a leg," Abraham Lincoln once said, "how many legs has a dog? Five? No; calling a tail a leg don't *make* it a leg." Words are simply functional parts of our logical machinery, helping us to translate sensory data into recognizable things. They perform no magic, yet without them our logical machinery simply wouldn't run.

Without our language we might still, like the apes, perceive the moon and the sun, but we could not see the moon as a "satellite" or the sun as a "star." The words which set us apart from our animal cousins focus our sensations into meaningful pictures in our minds. Words are thing-making tools; they are the hammer and tongs in what Shakespeare called "the quick forge and workinghouse of thought." With words, our most human possession, we fashion things in our minds from the same sensations available to our animal cousins; thus we live in a world of things to which they are almost entirely blind.

CHAPTER 3

The Role of Words in Qualification

Words help us to abstract qualities from things; to speak of greenness, for example, as something separate from grass or leaves. This act of taking qualities away from things is a symbolic process, not an "actual" one. You cannot really separate qualities from things, as you can parts. You can reach over and take away an apple's stem; the stem is a part. But you cannot reach over and take away the apple's redness; redness is a quality. In *Alice's Adventures in Wonderland,* the Cheshire Cat disappears except for its grin, which lingers in the air after the rest of it has gone. "Well!" says Alice, "I've often seen a cat without a grin . . . but a grin without a cat!" In the "real world" you cannot have greenness without grass or leaves; beauty without a woman or a sunset; melody without music; sweetness without sugar or a peach.

The mind is a different world. Symbolically you *can* separate qualities from things. When you say that two apples have the same red, you isolate the redness in your mind, something you cannot do with your fingers. With the word *grin* you mentally isolate the smile from the Cheshire Cat. In a sense, the redness and the grin float around by themselves in your consciousness. As we verbally abstract qualities from things, we create ghosts which float free of bodies. Thus we have "strength" separate from a muscular arm or steel bar; "blue" separate from the sky or blueberries; "speed" separate from running horses or flying airplanes; "accuracy" separate from shooting a rifle or adding a column of numbers. Symbolically, these qualities become "things" in their own right. The grins remain; the cats fade away.

Though our awareness of qualities is guided by the words we

use, we cannot, of course, experience qualities by means of words only. We cannot simply say "red" and see redness; we need eyes. (In imagination, however, the word alone may be enough.) For any quality that we experience, we must have a corresponding biological organ: eye, ear, nose, brain.

Our organs of consciousness enable us to experience three general types of qualities: sensory, emotional, and logical.

Let us first consider sensory qualities. These qualities exist for us because we have eyes, ears, a tongue, a nose, skin. We experience sensory qualities, and hence things, because we possess very complex sense organs which help create them for us. An apple becomes red when an eye sees it. An explosion becomes loud when an ear hears it. Ice cream becomes sweet when a tongue tastes it. A rose becomes fragrant when a nose smells it. A thorn becomes sharp when a finger touches it. If one of your sense organs is destroyed, the qualities it perceived are destroyed, too. Lose your eyes and apples lose redness; the apples you now feel or smell can only have the remembered redness of other apples. Lose your ears and explosions lose their loudness. The sensory qualities things have, for us, depend on the organs of sense we possess. If no one on Earth had eyes, there would be no redness for anyone. Would apples, then, be red?

The qualities we experience depend on our physical structure, the organs we have for interpreting light waves, air waves, chemical reactions. If we had other sense organs, in addition to the ones we now have, no doubt we would experience other qualities. Let us imagine that we had antennae on our heads which could detect X-rays and radio waves, which are now invisible to us. Would we not experience an aspect of the world now beyond our comprehension? Might we not experience things as unknowable to us now as the rainbow to a blind man? In addition to seeing the stars as we now see them, we might "hear" the stars which emit radio waves, the radio stars. We might "see" through walls, since radio waves and X-rays penetrate many solid objects, unlike light, which penetrates only a few solid objects: glass, ice, diamond, plastic. A concrete wall might make a very effective picture window. If you had antennae, you might see a lovely aurora borealis in a sky which is only a sky to the rest of us.

Who knows how many organs of sense may be possible if evolution permeates the universe? Perhaps beings living on a planet circling the star Polaris have one hundred sorts of sense organs, compared to our mere seven. How few the myriad possible qualities we may see! How limited our view of the world may be! How presumptuous of us to think that things as we see them are things as they "really are."

In addition to the ghost of redness, a rose may possess the ghost of beauty. Beauty, fear, anger, remorse, pity, love, hate: these are emotional qualities. Though we may have no specific organs of emotion, certainly emotions are in some way the result of our physical make-up. A snake can know no shame; a daisy can feel no fear; a horse cannot laugh or smile. Only humans have the human scope of emotions. Only we, on Earth, have the complexity of mental structure to know them. Perhaps a million years from now, if evolution continues its course, our ancestors will feel emotions as unknown to us as sorrow to a cockroach. One thing seems certain: emotional qualities reside in us, not in things. The beauty of the rose, like its color, is in our heads, not in the rose. As the saying goes, "Beauty is in the eye of the beholder."

There are logical ghosts as well as sensory and emotional ones. Indeed, to us real people, they are the most exalted ghosts of all. Size, shape, number, substance, change, time, space: these are basic logical qualities, qualities of relation which do not depend specifically on eye, ear, or feeling. The organ of logic is the brain. Only with a brain can we make comparisons, reach conclusions, see relations. Is a boulder "really" larger than a pebble? Perhaps, but this fact becomes "known" only if a brain makes the comparison. Perhaps, in "reality," there are six legs on a spider, but a spider doesn't know it. Only a human brain can count as high as six. Only a human brain can deduce that the sun is farther away from Earth than the moon. Only a human brain can predict the paths of planets, create machines and cities, chart the changing patterns of atoms, release on Earth the energy of stars. Our brains enable us to see these logical ghosts of things, these qualities of relation.

The brain is actually the controlling organ of all qualities that we experience. The brain seems to enable us to experience sensations and emotions as well as logical acts. We do not see sights in our eyes or hear sounds in our ears. Sensory organs merely transmit messages to the brain, which interprets them or not, as it chooses. If you are reading while someone is talking, you may not hear what he is saying. Though the sound waves reach your ears and are transmitted to your brain, you may not hear them, if your brain does not choose to accept them — to interpret and display them in consciousness. Our sense organs merely send impulses to the brain; the brain changes these impulses, as it chooses, into experiences. Emotions too seem subject to the brain, the ruling monarch of all we see and feel.

The brain appears to rule consciousness largely with symbols. Certainly words and other symbols play a vital role in shaping our experiences, in determining the qualities we see. A man walks through Washington, D.C. What does he see? "Much of the architecture is classical," he says. Could he see the quality "classical" without the help of words? In order to understand the similarity to early Greek and Roman architecture, must he not have read words in history books and listened to words spoken by history professors?

"The arms race seems to be accelerating," someone says. Could he see the quality of acceleration without words to help him out? Ask him what he means by "acceleration" and will he not explain in terms of other words, somewhat as follows: "Acceleration in a physical sense is positive change of rate, rate being distance divided by time. I am speaking figuratively. I don't mean that tanks or rockets are moving down a street or through the air at an increasingly faster speed. I mean that, like something physically accelerating, armament production is increasing not only in output but in *degree* of output." No doubt pictures go through his mind, pictures of moving cars, stockpiles of missiles and the like. But these pictures and these relations are called to consciousness by symbols. Certainly words are esssential to this thought, to the awareness of the quality "acceleration."

Though you may agree that complex logical qualities such as

"classical," "acceleration," "redundant," "vector," and "laissez-faire" may depend on symbols for your consciousness of them, you may feel that you can see the redness of a rose without words to help you out. Even if you can, aren't words useful devices even here? A laboratory animal can react to a red stimulus in a psychological experiment, but can it use a word to manipulate a "red ghost" in its mind? Can it, with a symbol such as *red,* manipulate redness imaginatively? Can it, like you, imagine redness overlaying a Christmas tree, and then with a spray gun actually *make* a red Christmas tree?

Imaginative, creative thinking is very much a matter of rearranging qualities with words, of mentally trying them in new combinations.

With the help of words and other symbols, we abstract qualities from things, making "ghosts" of them; with words we manipulate these ghosts, comparing, deducing, creating.

Qualities are the ingredients of the world's things. These qualities exist in our minds partly because we have sense organs, the capacity to feel emotions, and the brains to see relations. Partly they exist because we have the symbolic ability to abstract and manipulate them, to make sense of the data which come streaming into our brains.

CHAPTER 4

The Role of Words in Classification

Words help us to sort, to place similar things together in our minds, dividing them from dissimilar things. When we sort numerous items for a purpose, we are classifying. Words are the primary tools of sorting and of the complex, purposeful sorting we call classification. With the word *house* we sort into the same mental group similar objects which provide shelter: a brick structure in France, a wooden structure in England, a concrete structure in Nebraska. As we tie these like objects together, we at the same time exclude unlike objects: cathedrals, bridges, automobiles. The words we use in classification are the names of sorts, types, kinds, classes — things brought together because they are similar in some way.

The objects classified need not be "hooked together" in time or space — as Oregon is hooked to California and February is hooked to January. Our language gives us this special freedom. With class names we may group things together however we wish, according to any similarities we choose. Though Jimmy lived in Montana in 1956 and Bael lived in Norway in 1311, we may group them in the same "bad boy" class because we observe the similarity between them: "cause parents grief."

Classification involves the amazing symbolic capacity to arrange things in our minds differently from the way they are arranged in "reality." In a pasture, a cow is "actually" surrounded by grass, trees, a dog, insects. In the sea, a whale is "actually" surrounded by sharks, plankton, seaweed, submarines. However, in our minds we may place a cow and a whale in the same mental pasture (or sea): *mammals.* We see the similarities: "warm-blooded, suckle young"; and then put them in the same class by giving them the same name, *mammals* — transplanting them, as it were, into a new habitat. We classify primarily with words, placing things together by giving them the same name. We may lift the Matterhorn from the ice fields of Switzerland, the Kilimanjaro from the plains of Africa, and place them side by side in the same mental country: *mountains*. In this fashion we also place events or acts in classes. World War II is in the past, and we will look in vain for it in the world of today. Yet with the word *war* we can group it with other conflicts which may be further in the past or anticipated in the future. Possessing this symbolic ability to arrange whatever we wish however we wish, we can summon Plato from ancient Greece, fly Bertrand Russell from England, breathe life into the fictional Pangloss of dead Voltaire's imagination, and sit them down together in the same mental compartment: *philosophers*.

The words we use in classification normally bear a hierarchical relation to each other. That is, we classify objects by naming them on several levels, of more and more inclusive order. Charlie is a *boy*; a boy is a *child*; a child is a *human being*; a human being is an *animal*. Each successive level is larger than, and includes, the one below it. A larger, including level may be called a *genus*; a smaller, included level may be called a *species*. Boys are a species of the genus *children*; children are a species of the genus *human beings*; human beings are a species of the genus *animals*. Here is a diagram illustrating how we may classify objects in our minds by naming them on various levels, thus placing them in various genera and species:

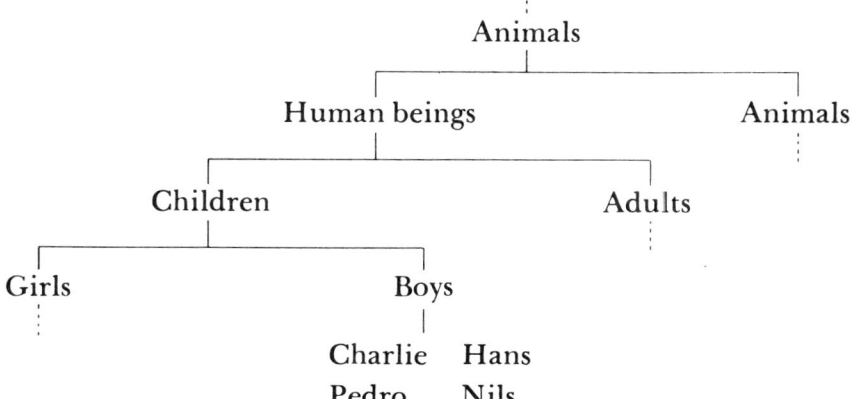

The words which indicate genera and species enable the mind to bring together into neat compartments things which literally may be scattered around the globe. This is the essence of classification: using words or other symbols to bring things together in new ways.

Words perform another very important function in classification. In addition to naming genera and species (that is, classes and sub-classes), words act as sorting factors. Sorting factors are of two types. One type is the name for the quality shared by the items in a group or class. The other type is the name for the type of quality *not* shared by the items in two or more groups or classes. That is, sorting factors are words which name the reasons we put things together or divide them apart. We put boys and girls together into the same genus *children* because they are similar in age. The word *young* would be a sorting factor, saying why we put them together. If we divide children into two species, *boys* and *girls, sex* is the word which tells why we divided them.

As we divide, we also put things together. As we divide children, we also put boys together and we put girls together. The sorting factor for boys is *male*; for girls, *female*. Thus when we say, or simply realize, that certain objects are children and that children are either boys or girls, we are working with four sorting factors: *young, sex, male,* and *female. Young, male,* and *female* name reasons for putting objects together. *Sex* names the reason for dividing objects apart.

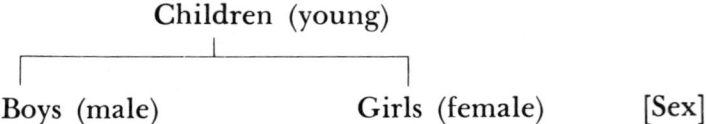

The concept of sorting factors is an important one, for whenever we classify we undergo this dual process of putting together and dividing apart. When we put whales, geraniums, and fleas together by calling them *organisms*, we are also dividing them from rocks, clouds, and bicycles, things which do not have life. When we divide organisms into plants and animals, we put ivy, grass, and junipers together under *plants,* and amoebas, cats, and salamanders together under *animals*. When you put all your pennies together in one pile, you necessarily divide them from the nickels, dimes, and quarters. It is a paradox, but nevertheless true, to say that dividing means putting together and that putting together means dividing. The two operations proceed simultaneously and interdependently, just as stars shine only when darkness surrounds them.

Sorting factors name the dual reasons for dividing and putting together. This is why we have two types of sorting factors: those which name similarities and those which name differences. What are the two types of sorting factors when you divide animals into animals, fish, and birds? *Location* may be the sorting factor naming differences, the reason for dividing animals into three groups: each group differs from the other in the location of its habitat, from land to water to air. *Water* may be one of the three sorting factors naming similarities: it names the reason for putting fish together; they live in water. *Land* may be the sorting factor naming the similarities between objects in the animal category. *Air* is the sorting factor naming the similarities among the objects in the bird class.

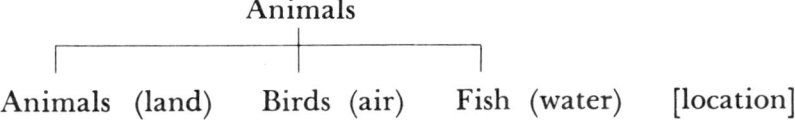

Animals (land)   Birds (air)   Fish (water)   [location]

Dividing and putting together by means of sorting factors is the basis of classification. These words give us the power to generalize, to reason, to deduce, to see the world as only we humans can. Seeing how things are similar and different is basic to human life, essential to consciousness. When we look out upon the world, what do we see? Can we make essential distinctions? Can we discover underlying similarities?

In Lewis Carroll's *Through the Looking Glass,* Alice is completely at a loss to distinguish between Tweedledum and Tweedledee. In *Alice's Adventures in Wonderland,* she is equally at a loss when asked, "Why is a raven like a writing-desk?" Are we good enough at classification to tell the difference between the Tweedledees and Tweedledums of our lives? Can we distinguish between one penny and another, one political party and another, one used car and another? Can we see, as Einstein saw, the minute but essential difference between time as measured by a clock on a moving train and time as measured by a clock in a stationary railway depot? "All that glitters is not gold," the saying goes. But many who can tell the difference between gold and fool's gold have great difficulty telling a good investment from a bad one.

How good are we at seeing what the ravens and writing desks of our lives have in common? What does a sprained ankle have in common with a quarrel? How about "poor planning" or "lack of caution"? Asking this question and getting a good answer might lead to corrective measures, preventing not only future sprains and quarrels, but other "mishaps" as well.

What does a train whistle have in common with starlight? Without a question such as this, and an appropriate answer (both move in a wave-like pattern), modern physics would not be what it is today. Newton saw that an apple falls to Earth, and the moon doesn't, for the same reason: gravitation. He was able to see the undercurrent of similarity amid obvious diversity. He was good at classification, at sorting things according to similarities and differences. Einstein went one step beyond him when he saw what a falling apple and a ray of light have in common.

In order to become better classifiers, we must realize what may not at first seem apparent: words are the primary tools we use. We must understand that without our language, the symbolic heritage of centuries, we would be at a loss to see things as *types* of things; we would not observe similarities and differences. There would be no store of knowledge bequeathed to us from the past; we could not add to the store of knowledge during our lifetimes. If we lacked speech, as do our nearest cousins, the apes, we might be fighting *them* for *Lebensraum*.

CHAPTER 5

The Role of Words in Structure Analysis

Words help us to see how an object is physically put together, though, of course, diagrams and similar devices also help in this kind of analysis. The words *root, trunk,* and *leaves* help us to think about the parts of a tree. The words *back, seat,* and *legs* help us to think about the parts of a chair. The words *skull, spine, ribs,* and *clavicle* help us to analyze the parts of a skeleton.

In order to appreciate the role of words in structure analysis, we must realize that wholes and parts are mental phenomena which shift their boundaries as we shift our thoughts. There is no such thing as a "real" whole or a "real" part. Wholes and parts are relative entities which we delineate symbolically in our minds.

A whole is simply the largest spatial thing we are concerned with at the moment of analysis. Every whole can be part of something larger. A rose is a whole which we can divide into parts such as petals, stem, and leaves; but if we shift our attention to a higher level, the rose becomes a *part* of a rosebush. The rosebush is now the whole, because it is the largest thing in which we have interest. We can, of course, go up and up as we shift our level of interest. The rosebush is a part of the whole garden; the garden is a part of the whole Earth; the Earth is a part of the whole solar system; the solar system is a part of the whole universe. (The universe is the only whole which cannot be a part of something else.)

Going downwards from the rose, one of its petals can be a whole if we are concerned with *its* parts — cells; the cells can be wholes, composed of atoms; the atoms can be wholes, composed of electrons, protons, and other elementary particles.

From electrons below to the universe above there is a spectrum of shifting concepts: parts become wholes, wholes become parts, whenever we shift the level of our attention. In one direction, we shatter Humpty Dumpty into fragments; in the other direction we combine the fragments into larger wholes. This principle of attentional, hierarchic relativity is true of all forms of analysis.

We do this dividing into parts and combining into wholes at mental "joints," places of division which we choose. The parts and wholes of the world really exist in our heads; they are whatever our symbols make them. How many parts does the object below have? In order to decide, you must mentally cut it apart. These "cuts" are like the joints between bones; they are places of division.

Five, you say? Or three? The drawing is a stylized copy of the Great Lakes, which has five parts, as everyone knows. But why five? Are the waters actually divided into five separate units? No land separates them from each other. It is especially evident that the leftmost three are one body of water. The dividing lines are purely imaginary, mental projections. The divisions between the lakes are not dictated by nature, but are imposed by human intelligence. We may divide structures into whatever parts we like.

The "joints" at which we divide structures into parts are always a result of human choice. Often these joints are purely imaginary, seemingly arbitrary. What "real" line, or joint, separates Arizona from New Mexico? What river, mountain range, or fissure in the earth? None; the line is a human invention, a mental projection. Are not property lines and the equator arbitrary divisions also? If you were to divide an iceberg, floating in the sea, into two parts, where would you draw the line? Wouldn't you imaginatively project the surface of the sea through the solid ice? Whenever you speak, or simply think, of a mountain rising from a plain, you project a mental division where there is no "actual" break in the continuous earth. The eyeball seems to have a distinct "joint" dividing it from the rest of the head. The spherical enclosure in which the eye moves seems to be the obvious dividing place. Yet the optic nerve is connected to the eyeball and travels to the brain. Are the eyeball and the brain one part then? If we are to say that the eyeball is a part separate from the brain, must we not mentally cut through the optic nerve? When you think of an unborn child separate from the mother that holds it in her womb, you mentally cut through the umbilical cord before the doctor does so actually.

Some "joints," in contrast to state lines and such, seem real: the joint between two bones, the "joint" between the head and handle of a hammer. In a sense, though these joints are "actual," we create them too, just as we create imaginary joints. Structure analysis is a symbolic process. We are free to divide structures into parts however we wish. We choose our own places of division.

A printer makes "real" divisions between the signatures (physical sections) of a book; yet we, the readers, can ignore them, dividing the book instead into chapters. You ignore the natural division between the skin and insides of an orange when you say, "The left half is rotten." You imaginatively slice the fruit into two halves.

We choose whatever joints we wish, ignoring others. We can choose "real" joints, rejecting other real joints. We can choose imaginary ones, rejecting real ones. Because we choose, we *create* the joints of the structures we analyze.

If you were to divide this drawing into two parts, where would you draw the line?

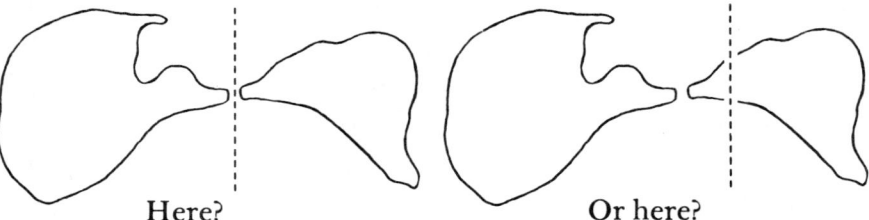

Here?   Or here?

Where do we draw the line between Central America and South America? At the Panama Canal, a physical boundary? No, at nothing in particular, two hundred miles beyond! As symbol-using creatures, we are free to dissect the world around us however we please. Some of us have "good" reasons; others disagree.

Like all rational thought, structure analysis involves the use of words and other symbols. By this process of "representing" spatial entities in our heads, we in a sense "create" the structures we analyze. Is there "really" a United States, separate from our thoughts about it? Shorelines define the eastern and western borders, but what demarcations separate America from Canada and Mexico? Aren't these southern and northern boundaries purely mental lines which human beings draw and agree upon? In fact, the shorelines are mental creations too, drawn amid the shifting tides with words or maps and charts. We cannot notice a shoreline until we symbolize it. "Whenever there is a sea," writes Albert Upton in *Design for Thinking*, "somebody must say to the water, so far you go and no farther; and to the land he must say, this is the end of you." The waters rush in and recede, never resting. Is there ever an actual shoreline? Must we not symbolize a shoreline, amidst the ebb and flood? "A person must draw that line somewhere," writes Upton.

Symbolically, we create our own boundaries. By means of words such as *land, sea,* and *America* (manipulated in conjunction with maps, charts, and other representations) we "draw" the United States in our minds. Once symbolically "created" (that is, divided from surrounding spaces), it may be subdivided into constituent parts — with the help of words such as *state, county, city, Florida,* and *Chicago.* The words help us to locate parts and parts within parts.

Words give us the power to "create" and analyze aspects of reality to which we were formerly blind. In Aristotle's mind, there was no central nervous system. Biologists of a later age named certain elements and thus "created" it and divided it into parts, with words such as *brain, neurone, synapse, dendrite,* and *cortex.* With language as a vehicle of structural thought, astronomers have created a new universe, made of planets, solar systems, and galaxies — quite a different structure from the earlier universe, made of Earth, Heaven, Hell, and Purgatory.

The symbolic nature of structure analysis becomes even more apparent when we realize that there are no structures to analyze, really. There are only operations. The world never stands still. We must stop it (make structures out of it) symbolically. You must stop a ticking clock in order to take it apart. If you are to think of a human being as a structure composed of a skeleton, muscles, a circulatory system, you must stop the person in your mind. You must symbolize a static structure, where there is "really" a walking, talking, living person. Even if you analyze a corpse, you must mentally create a static structure. For a corpse is an operation too. It deteriorates; electrons swirl around the nuclei of its atoms; it swishes around in the formaldehyde tank as you cut into it. All structures are mental creations, made with words and other symbols.

We comprehend the complexities of spatial organization largely because words enable us to signify wholes, parts, and parts within parts.

CHAPTER 6

The Role of Words in Operation Analysis

Words facilitate the comprehension of happenings and their stages. With the word *day* we compress a twenty-four-hour period into a moment of consciousness; with the words *morning, afternoon,* and *night* we think of the constituent stages, or "time parts," of the total period. Words enable us to experience and divide happenings which would otherwise, because of their great duration, extend beyond our vision.

We live in a world too vast to grasp in the "present moment." At any one time, we can glimpse only a brief span of duration, only a small segment of the endless scroll. Perhaps an infinite mind, a God, could comprehend all happenings in a single gigantic experience, seeing at the same time though in perfect succession the events of yesterday, the Civil War, the Ice Ages, the creation of the Earth.

Our span of present awareness is much shorter. If someone repeats a random series of numbers aloud, we can remember about seven or eight. The earlier numbers begin to escape our memory, to fade into the past. All experiences have a similarly brief duration. We eat a peach, and at the third bite the experience of the first is gone. As we listen to a song, old notes vanish into the past almost as soon as new ones reach our ears. When we see where a moving car now is, we no longer see where it was. William James describes the moment of present awareness as "a sort of saddle-back of time with a certain length of its own, on which we sit perched, and from which we look in two directions into time." Beyond the edges of this narrow saddle-back, we are blind, except in memory. Present experiences vanish over the edge. The "now" is a bright inch in a million dark miles. And the somewhat disconcerting fact is that the past is "real" only when *re*collected in the present and that the future never "was" and may not necessarily ever "be."

If all that we can experience of the operational world must fit within the inch of the "now," how can we know anything of yesterday, of events which have ceased to occur? We keep these events alive with words and other symbols. Words stimulate memories of past events, or thoughts of imagined events. The words *day, morning, afternoon,* and *night* gather into our present experience recollections of rising suns, bright days, and starry skies. By means of words such as *birth, life, death; ancient, medieval, modern* we in a sense see beyond the edges of our temporal saddle (backward over the cantle and forward over the pommel), assembling in the mind's eye pictures of newborn children, schoolyards, weddings, funerals; pyramids under construction, coronations, factories in operation — events we are not directly experiencing. With words we bind time into our inch of vision, seeing representative glimpses of complex occurrences.

This process can be likened to fitting a large number of jelly beans into a small jar. Imagine that you have one hundred pounds of red jelly beans, one hundred pounds of yellow ones, and one hundred pounds of green ones. You cannot put all the jelly beans, all three hundred pounds, into the jar at once. But you can "represent" them all by filling the jar with a mixture of a few red ones, a few yellow ones, and a few green ones. In a similar way we fit long happenings into the "small jar" of our present experience.

Genesis begins with the general statement, "In the beginning God created the heaven and the earth." These words "represent" the seven days, which may be likened to seven different colors of jelly beans. They call to mind a mixture of representative impressions: a flash of light, Earth materializing in the midst of blankness, stars coming to life in the void. These representative events stand for the total event, which, in its entirety, is too complex to be comprehended all at once. We cannot think about all the happenings of all seven days at one time.

Once we have a general impression of the total operation, we can proceed to examine in detail certain stages of the operation. We may fill the jar with red jelly beans; then we may empty it of the red ones and fill it with yellow ones; and so on, thinking about shorter periods of time in greater detail. We may think in detail about just the first day of Creation (not about all seven days). Our minds (our jars) may be filled with "red jelly bean" thoughts — perhaps impressions of a bearded Jehovah saying, "Let there be light," a sudden brightness, a division of the brightness from the darkness. This is all our minds can take in at once. We must empty our minds of these impressions before we can take in "yellow jelly bean" thoughts — thoughts of the appearance of dry land and seas, the growth of grass, herbs, fruit trees.

Thus we think about successive stages of an operation: filling the mind (the "present moment"), emptying it, refilling it, and so on. If we wish to think of two or more stages at once (a broader, inclusive stage), we must select and mix red and yellow jelly beans; or red, yellow, green, blue, orange, and brown jelly beans. The longer and more complex the operation, the more general our thought must be, the more sparse our selection of representative events (the fewer of each color of jelly bean).

Our language is the symbolic medium which enables us to think in this fashion, to shift from detailed thoughts of short happenings to general thoughts of long happenings. With the words "God created the heaven and the earth" we create in our minds a long, general happening. At the next moment we may, with the words "God created great whales," create a more detailed, shorter happening. It is in this symbolic fashion that we expand our vision beyond the narrow saddle-back "on which we sit perched." With our language we, unlike animals which are without speech, create operations and their stages; thus in a short space of time we perceive happenings, long and short. Thus we live in a wide world with echoes from the past and intimations of the future.

In the poem "Go and Catch a Falling Star," John Donne says, "Tell me where all past years are." Perhaps we can never know where they "really are"; but for us they exist in memory. With words and other symbols we erect mental signposts in our minds, thus marking off events, thus storing away "all past years."

It seems clear that operations *as we know them* are compressed, symbolized entities. In our minds, we represent them; then we may analyze them, dividing them with words into time elements, or stages.

What an operation or a stage "is" depends not on the external world, but upon the mind's *view* of the external world. Operations do not come to us like bread, pre-packaged and pre-sliced. Something we conceive to be an operation at one moment can become a stage at the next, and vice versa. A day is an operation which we can divide into the stages day and night; but if we shift our attention to a more lengthy interval, a day can become a stage of a week. The week is now the operation, because it is the longest thing with which we are concerned. The week can cease being an operation and become a stage if we shift our attention to a month.

Every operation can become a stage of something more inclusive, as our thoughts lengthen in time. We can go from month to year to decade to millennium. In the other direction, a stage can always become an operation, if our thinking shrinks in time. A day (opposite of night) is a stage of a day (twenty-four hours). But the daylight period shifts from a stage to an operation if our attention becomes centered only on it. Its stages may be morning and afternoon. Morning, in turn, may change from a stage to an operation if we become concerned only with it and *its* stages. Stages and operations are relative entities. We can cut the cake of the operational world however we wish. Of course, we use words and other symbols to do the cutting.

The identification of operations and stages is very largely a verbal process, dictated by the mind, not by an external reality which is already divided. With symbols *we* decide how to divide operations into "time-parts," just as we decide at what "joints" to cut structures into spatial parts. A caterpillar dies for every butterfly that is born; the child dissolves into the man. Symbols enable us to make these divisions; that is, when we name stages of operations, we understand each stage to have an end, which is the beginning of the next stage. These "beginning-ends" may be called junctures.

Junctures, or "time-joints," sometimes seem natural, sometimes contrived. In any case, it is we who decide where the dividing points shall be, just as it is we who decide where to cut the turkey or where to divide Mexico from the United States. Sunset seems a natural juncture between afternoon and night. But where is the natural division between youth and manhood? In some states, lawmakers have decided on twenty-one years of age; in others, eighteen. A caterpillar becomes a butterfly quickly and dramatically; we feel impelled to make this "dividing-time" the juncture between two main stages of the one organism. How natural is the division between January and February? No natural phenomenon signals a change. For our own purposes, we have invented arbitrary boundaries. What point separates life from death? Doctors, judges, and clergymen have their own methods of deciding. "I am convinced the spirit had not left him," a priest might say. Regardless of how natural and obvious junctures may seem, it is we who decide where to draw the time lines.

In summary, this is what we do in operation analysis: with symbols we compress happenings into our "inch" of consciousness; with symbols we define operations, stages, and sub-stages; with symbols we designate the junctures (or points of division) between stages or between sub-stages.

The salient fact to bear in mind is that to a very large extent words make operation analysis possible. The following outline represents an operation, its stages, and its sub-stages. As you read it, you will see that you cannot comprehend all of it in complete detail at one time. You must shift your attention from element to element. The words and their relation to each other stand on paper as reminders, to stimulate thoughts in your mind as you read them. But you cannot read them all at once; you cannot see at the same time all of the pictures which they are capable of stimulating in your mind. You must shift from statement to statement, from one specific thought to another specific thought;

or from a specific thought to a general thought. The words act as markers, remaining in place so that you may return to that which you have already comprehended.

    HUNTING
        I. Stalking
            A. Tracking
            B. Sighting
            C. Approaching
       II. Shooting
            A. Aiming
            B. Firing
                1. Squeezing of trigger
                2. Explosion of charge
                3. Recoil and flight of bullet
            C. Wounding or killing of game
      III. Retrieving

With words as markers, reminders, stimulators of thought, we may from moment to moment control operations much too vast to comprehend at once. With words and other symbols, we think in general and then in particular, then in general again, then in particular, and in even more particular, and so on. In this way we comprehend the past, make plans for the future, record transactions, keep track of changing events on graphs and charts, plan invasions, invent rockets, regulate commerce and government.

With our human capacity for speech, we think of happenings in general; we break them into stages and sub-stages. In this fashion, by linking one moment of consciousness to another, we can control operations of incredible duration and complexity. We can learn the secrets of growth, planting seeds in the spring and harvesting grain in the fall; we can discover the hidden properties of matter, creating steel and fashioning it in complex living factories; we can divine the mysteries of human nature, inventing social systems for controlling it and freeing it to grow and create; we can learn the ways of suns, moons, and atoms, devising fantastic schemes for reaching into space. On Earth, only man can plan such operations. And he can do so only with words, numbers, charts, and other symbolic images — things which bring other things to mind. We will achieve the stars and a better world not by evolving wings but by evolving a better understanding of the symbolic heritage by which we have climbed thus far.

CHAPTER 7

The Role of Words in Analogy

Words help us to comprehend similar relations in different worlds of thought — to see analogies. "Necessity is the mother of invention." This arrangement of words helps us to see that necessity motivates invention just as a mother bears a child; something causes an end result. The statement shows that a relation in the world of child-rearing is similar to a different relation in the world of inventing. Two views from two different worlds are made to coincide. The two views are brought together and focused, as it were, by the words of the sentence: *necessity, mother, invention.*

An analogy seems to inhabit two worlds, but actually inhabits three. We start out with two worlds, but by focusing on their similarities we create a third "overworld." Words and other symbols bring two relations together into one larger relation, just as the power of sight focuses two pictures into one comprehensive picture. When the view from the right eye coincides with the view from the left eye, the mind sees a third view, in depth. Analogies are mental stereopticons.

When we read the words, "Necessity is the mother of invention," what do we see? With our "left eye" we see a mother bearing a child. With our "right eye" we see necessity motivating someone to invent something. When these two views coincide into one greater one, we see in more universal perspective something preceding and causing an outcome. This general relation "hovers over" the two lesser ones. With words guiding our thoughts, we "see" an analogy with three minds: two minds which perceive relations, and a third and wiser mind which combines the relations into a greater whole of deeper consciousness.

An analogy may be analyzed in diagrammatic form, as follows: "Necessity is the mother of invention."

World of Child Rearing	World of General Conception	World of Inventing
A. Mother	Initial Entity	C. Necessity
bears	causes	motivates
B. Child	End Result	D. Invention

Notice that the word *mother* shifts from the world of child-rearing to the world of inventing, thus bringing to life the new concept. When a word travels by the route of analogy, it is a prince that enters the silent forest of the unrealized, awakening the sleeping beauty of fresh insight.

All of us send words to new mental lands, sparking new meanings in our minds. When we send the word *coat* from the world of clothing to the world of paint, we create the meaning "coat of paint." When we send the word *bath* from the world of human hygiene to the world of photography, we create the meaning "chemical bath for negatives and prints." When we send the word *branch* from the world of trees to the world of commerce, we create the meaning "branch of a department store." The common words of English travel constantly, from land to land.

Words stimulate the perception of analogous relations at every level of thought and in every area of our lives. Writers, scientists, and all other thinkers create new insights by analogy, using words to relate diverse phenomena. In one of his speeches, Herbert Hoover said, "Absolute freedom of the press... is a foundation stone of American liberty," expressing the idea that freedom of the press is *at the bottom of* and *holds up* the rest of American freedom, just as a foundation stone supports other stones of a building. Thomas Moore focuses our attention on the similarity between infinite space and infinite time when he writes, "This narrow isthmus 'twixt two boundless seas / The past, the future,—two eternities!" Scientists use the word *wave* to conceptualize the mathematical similarity between patterns of condensation in air (sound "waves") and patterns of undulation in water. A biologist may speak of one cell breaking off from another as a "daughter" cell. Chemists and physicists, in their thinking, transfer the word *shell* from the world of nuts and shellfish to the world of atoms, allowing them to conceptualize "shells" of electrons around a nucleus.

Whenever something new is invented, conceived, created—whether a work of art, a mechanical device, a scientific principle, or what have you—analogies are likely to be among the mental tools used in the achievement. For analogies are among the most basic implements of our minds, operating at all levels, from the semiconscious to the highly creative. Words and other symbols make these analogous thoughts possible, showing broad general relations among seemingly unrelated relations of a lower level.

CHAPTER 8

Ambiguity: Some Words Have Many Meanings

Now we come to a paradox. Words and other symbols, the tools of analysis, perform their guiding function with a seeming handicap. They are often ambiguous; they can mean different things at different times. *Red* may mean what blood is or what Russians, Chinese, and Cubans are; *current* may refer to flowing water, electricity, or the latest news; *run* may signify what a quarterback does with his feet, a politician does in his campaign, an automobile engine does with its piston and rods, or what a woman has in her stocking.

Not all words are ambiguous. *Hemialgia, nonagon, soffit, ballista, wot:* these and thousands like them have a single recorded meaning each. In contrast, most of the words we use most often possess a surprisingly high number of things and thoughts to which they may refer. The words *man, tree, watch, fan,* and *circle* have more than ten meanings apiece. The words *make, light, point, line,* and *turn* have over fifty senses each. The word *set* has more than two hundred.

This basic characteristic of language is frequently overlooked. Too often people expect words to have single "proper" meanings. *Head* "really" means the thing on a man's shoulders; *book* "really" means a thing with pages. Few people are fully aware of the large clusters of meanings surrounding our most common (and most useful) words.

What is a *head*? "The top part of a human being" is the meaning which most readily comes to mind. This is what the Queen of Hearts in *Alice's Adventures in Wonderland* meant when she shouted, "Off with his head!" Queen Elizabeth had the same meaning in mind when she said in equally ominous tones, "I will make you shorter by the head." But when Disraeli said to Queen Victoria, "Your majesty is the head of the literary profession," he meant the *whole* of her. A "head of hair" is something on *top* of a head; a "good head for figures" is something *inside* the head. When we speak of the head of a pin, the head of an arrow, the head of a glass of beer, the head of a page, the head of a bed, or the head of a class, we mean something which (like a man's head) is the top or foremost of something, yet may not resemble a man's head in other respects. A head of cabbage resembles a man's head only in shape and size; the head of a coin may have a man's head stamped on it (but who ever saw the "tail" of a coin with a tail on it?); much more distant similarity is to be found in the boil or crisis which comes to a head. Clustered around a key sense of the word are many related meanings, some near, some far — yet all different.

What is a *book*? Does this word mean only an object like the one you are now holding? Like *head*, it is surrounded by a cluster of related meanings. The Bible is a book, but so are Genesis, Exodus, Deuteronomy, and the other "books" of the Bible. You might say that the Book of Books is literally a "book of books." Your personal copy of the Bible is a book, but when you say, "The Bible is a great book," you are speaking of quite a different thing, not of a single copy but of the "Bible in general" — all the copies in the world, so to say. Can there be a book without words or pages? What about a book of matches, a book of cards, or the book of life? If we were all to agree on a single meaning for the word *book*, which should we choose? How about this definition, set down by the United States Copyright Office:

> The term "books" covers not only material published in book form, but also pamphlets, leaflets, cards, and single pages containing text. Books include fiction, nonfiction, poetry, collections, directories, catalogs, and information in tabular form.

A single printed page is a book! (In one sense.)

Words can have as many different senses as we wish to give them. Even numbers, the so-called "constants" of mathematics, have multiple meanings. The number *10*, for example, often means something quite different from "ten" of something. It can mean tenth in a series (as, the *single* horse which finished the race after the horse which finished ninth); it can mean "Number 10" (the horse which may have finished first); it can mean a playing card marked with the number *10*; it can mean a ten-dollar bill. In binary mathematics (the arithmetic of many computers), *10* means two. In the octal numbering system, *10* means nine. When used as a code, *10* can mean anything you want it to mean. In a two-digit code for classifying clothes in a stockroom, the numbers 0, 1, 2, and 3, on the left, might stand for men's, women's, girls', and boys', respectively. The numbers 0, 1, 2, and 3, on the right, might stand for red, yellow, blue, and green, respectively. Thus *10* would stand for a woman's red garment. In commerce, industry, and science, there are thousands of coding systems in which *10* might mean anything from copper nails to delinquent accounts receivable. There need not be "ten" of anything associated with any of these meanings. All other numbers are similarly ambiguous.

Ambiguity is a basic characteristic of words, numbers, mathematical signs, diagrams, charts, and all other symbols — things which stand for things. "When *I* use a word," says Humpty Dumpty in *Through the Looking Glass,* "it means just what I choose it to mean — neither more nor less." Words and all other symbols can mean whatever we wish them to mean, and can change their meanings as we change our thoughts. Any symbol can become ambiguous, if it is not already so. As you might surmise, *ambiguity* is itself ambiguous and as used here does not refer to vagueness or uncertainty of meaning but to the fact that symbols may be used — and properly and precisely used — in two or more different senses.

CHAPTER 9

How Words Change Their Meanings

Words and other symbols are not born ambiguous; they become so through use. As we shift them to new contexts, where they take on new meanings, they become increasingly ambiguous.

All symbols are mental chameleons: they can take on new shades of meaning whenever you place them in new surroundings. Consider the word *glass*. When placed in the sentence, "Mirrors are made of _____," it means a substance, the material silicon dioxide, not a thing with shape or size. When shifted to the sentence, "My _____ is empty," *glass* now means a drinking glass, an object with size and shape, something capable of being empty, unlike a formless substance. When further shifted to the sentence, "There is only a _____ of wine left in the bottle," the word *glass* now stands for a quantity, a volume, not a solid or a material; it stands for the amount of something which can be contained in a drinking glass.

Nonlinguistic symbols behave as chameleons too, when shifted from context to context. In the formula 3 X 5 = 15, the X means "times" or "multiplied by." When transferred to the phrase "a 3 X 5 card," it comes to mean "by," signifying not that two numbers should be multiplied but that they should be interpreted as the two dimensions of a rectangular object.

As a symbol moves from context to context, it may change its meaning as surely as a chameleon changes its color when it walks from a green forest to a yellow desert. New areas of thought demand new meanings.

Ambiguity is not a necessary evil, something to be minimized or eliminated; it is an essential good. As symbols change their meanings, new thoughts are born. There is a profound relation between the nature of ambiguity and the process of thought. Seldom do words and other symbols acquire new meanings in a completely random fashion. Ordinarily they become ambiguous or increasingly ambiguous along definite routes or paths. These are the very same avenues along which thoughts travel: the mental phases of THING-MAKING, QUALIFICATION, CLASSIFICATION, STRUCTURE ANALYSIS, OPERATION ANALYSIS, and ANALOGY.

Sense Growing via Thing-Making

The name of a thing may be transferred to another thing which resembles it in some way. Let us assume that the word *corona* originally means a crown, as worn by a king. Someone looks at the halo around the sun during an eclipse and calls it a *corona,* because it resembles a crown. The name of nearly anything may be shifted to something like it, regardless of how abstract the similarity may be. Why was the cloud of smoke resulting from an atomic blast called a mushroom? Someone observed its similarity to a vegetable mushroom. If you were the first man to observe the luminous streak following a comet, what would you call it? Wouldn't you call it a tail because of its resemblance to the tail of an animal?

The resemblance between two things, resulting in a verbal shift, need not be visual. Because of an auditory similarity, the word *babble,* meaning what a baby does, may come to mean what a stream does. The observed similarities between things have resulted in sense growths beyond counting: *eye* of a person to *eye* of a needle; *arrow* of an Indian to *arrow* on a diagram; *tongue* in mouth to *tongue* in shoe; *furrows* in plowed field to *furrows* in worried forehead; *squeak* of a mouse to *squeak* of new shoes; *star* (brilliant object) in sky to *star* ("brilliant" person) in movies; *cloverleaf* in meadow to *cloverleaf* in highway intersection; *saucer* in cupboard to flying *saucer* in sky.

Sense Growth via Qualification

The name of a thing may be transferred to one of its qualities or the name of a quality may be transferred to a thing possessing it. If you speak of an orange on a tree and then of orange, the color of sunset, you shift the name of the fruit to one of its qualities: orangeness. The word *youth* may mean the quality of being young. At the next moment the word may become the name of a thing having youthfulness: a young man, *a youth*. If someone thinks of the bow (or bend) in a piece of wood and then of a bow, the device for shooting arrows, he symbolizes first a quality and then a thing possessing that quality.

Hundreds of English words shift from thing to quality, quality to thing: *green* (the color of grass) to the village *green;* *sun* in the sky to *sun* on the building; a *foot* with toes to a *foot* with inches.

Sense Growth via Classification

By the process of classification, we often move words up and down the scale of generalization. A word thus shifted includes more than or less than in its previous sense. You may say, "All men are mortal." *Man,* in a former statement meaning "adult males," now means "human beings, *including* females and children," a more inclusive class. Words often become less general rather than more. A person learns that a pyramid is any solid object with a square base and triangular sides which meet at a common point. He then learns about the Egyptian pyramids. The meaning of *pyramid* narrows to include only the tombs in Egypt; it no longer, in this context, includes *all* objects of this shape.

Hundreds of words freely and naturally shift their boundaries of meaning, including now more objects, now fewer: *plant,* any member of the vegetable kingdom, including trees, to *plant,* only soft-stemmed "plants"; *cow,* the female of any bovine animal, to *cow,* the female of many large animals, such as the buffalo, elephant, and whale; *sun,* the star around which Earth moves, to *sun,* the center of any solar system; *moon,* Earth's satellite, to *moon,* the satellite of any planet, as a moon of Mars; *artist,* one who paints, to *artist,* anyone who creates, as, "a great literary artist"; *glass,* a drinking implement made of glass, to *glass,* any drinking implement, regardless of its substance, as, "a plastic glass."

Sense Growth via Structure Analysis

A word may shift in meaning from a whole to a part or from a part to a whole. You may refer to your hand and then to a ranch hand, transferring the meaning of *hand* from a part of a person to a whole person. You shift from whole to part when you first speak of a flower growing in the ground, and then say, "I plucked the flower from the stem." *Flower* now means just the blossom, not the whole plant. Ireland is an island, composed of two parts: the independent nation of Ireland, and Northern Ireland, which is a part of Great Britain. The word *Ireland* can shift back and forth, as you use it, from island to nation, nation to island: whole to part, part to whole. If a person first learns that *earth* means dirt and then our whole planet Earth, he moves a word from a part of a structure to an entire structure.

Many words shift in this structural manner: *train* behind an engine to *train,* including the engine; *body,* the torso or midsection of a man, to *body,* a man's entire "body," as opposed to his soul; *page,* one side of a printed sheet (as, "page 37") to *page,* an entire leaf (including both sides, pages 37 and 38); *seat,* part of a chair, to *seat,* an entire chair (as, "Pull up a seat"); *God,* the Father, to *God* "in three persons," the Trinity (Father, Son, and Holy Ghost); *peanut,* the plant growing in the ground, to *peanut,* a salted nut in a jar; *world,* the Earth, to *world,* the universe.

Sense Growth via Operation Analysis

Words often shift in meaning from one element of an operation to another. *Land* means ground, the earth. The word takes on a new sense when you say that an airplane lands. Thinking operationally, you transfer the name of a location to a happening which involves the location. The Bible provides a good example of shift in verbal meaning along operational lines. "God called the light day, and the darkness he called night. And the evening and the morning were the first day." The word *day*, meaning opposite of night, shifts to include night too, a total twenty-four-hour period, "day." In Shakespeare's "To be or not to be" soliloquy, the word *death* shifts operationally in Hamlet's mind. Hamlet first mentions the "sleep of death," meaning the period after one dies, between death and judgment. Then he expresses his "dread of something after death." *Death* is now the *point* of dying, the "bourne" or boundary line "from which no traveller returns" — not the period after dying.

Operational sense growths include all shifts of meaning back and forth between operations, stages, and parts in the context of happenings. Here are a few examples: *fish* in stream to *fish* for trout; to *act* in a play to *Act* I; *dance* with a partner to graduation *dance*; *football*, the ball, to *football*, the game; *time*, a length of duration, to *time*, the present moment, as, "Do you have the time?"; *saw* hanging on the nail to *saw* the wood; *milk* in a glass to *milk* the cow; *step*, a stride, to *step* made of wood; *paint* in a can to *paint* the house; *moon*, Earth's satellite, to *moon*, a lunar month; *sound*, a noise which may be loud, to *sound*, vibrations in air which cause noise in the mind.

SENSE GROWTH VIA ANALOGY

By the process of analogy (or metaphor, as it is often called), words shift in meaning to show new relations in new worlds of thought. We see that A is to B as C is to D. The word *root* means the underground base of a plant. By analogy, the word *root* grows a new sense when used in the sentence, "Love of money is the root of all evil." Transferred from the world of growing things to the world of human actions, the word gains a new sense, showing that love of money is a basic cause of the origin of evil just as a biological root is a basic cause of the growth of a plant. A branch is a limb of a tree. *Branch* shifts meaning by analogy when you speak of a branch of a company. A branch is to the trunk of the tree as the "branch office" is to the main office of the company. An exit is a door leading out of a building. A computer programmer, when he speaks of an exit, shifts his thinking by analogy to this new sense: "instruction which transfers processing out of a sub-routine." A is to B as C is to D: a computer leaves the sub-routine through an "exit" instruction as a person leaves the building through the exit. (Originally *exit* was a whole Latin sentence meaning "he goes out.") Here are examples of other words which often shift their senses by the route of analogy: *artery*, carrying blood, to traffic *artery*, carrying automobiles; *fruit* on a tree to *fruit* of labor; *jacket* of a boy to *jacket* on a book; *weave* a sweater to *weave* a tale; *field* for plowing to *field* of chemistry.

SENSE GROWTH VIA MISCELLANEOUS ROUTES

Words do not always grow new senses precisely along the routes of thing-making, qualification, classification, structure analysis, operation analysis, and analogy. Sometimes they appear to shift their senses along a combination of two or more of these routes. The word *pound* means something a hammer does. How does this word grow when you say, "The sea pounds"? Probably by a combination of thing-making and analogy. The sea *sounds* like a hammer pounding. Also, the sea beats against the shore as a hammer hits an object: A is to B as C is to D.

If you shift the word *water* from the liquid to the general substance (including ice and water vapor), what route does your mind follow? Possibly a combination of classification, structure analysis, and operation analysis. You might think of water, water vapor, and ice as different classes of "water." In addition, you might think of water as it is physically located on Earth's surface, part vapor in clouds, part liquid in oceans and lakes, part solid in icebergs and polar caps. Also, operation analysis might play a role in the verbal shift: you might think of the *process* by which water changes its states — changing, with the application of heat, from ice to water to water vapor.

Though sometimes the reasons for verbal shifts may be difficult to determine, only very rarely do words gain new senses for no apparent reasons at all. *Glory,* said Humpty Dumpty in *Through the Looking Glass,* means "there's a nice knock-down argument for you!" You may, if you wish, arbitrarily let *tree* mean bicarbonate of soda. But ordinarily you and all other rational human beings, shift words to new senses for reasons. You see some relation between old and new. This relation can usually be identified as one or a combination of the six non-symbolic phases of thought.

Our language, together with other kinds of symbols we have invented, appears to be a gigantic mirror of the intellect. The processes of progressive ambiguity (sense growth) reflect the processes of thought. We see new meanings for words and other symbols in the same ways that we think new thoughts.

Perhaps these two phenomena are more closely related than we realize. Perhaps we cannot think new thoughts *unless* we see new meanings for words and other symbols. Perhaps the processes of thinking and symbolic sense growth are one and the same: a single caravan, not two; dual tributaries of one river, not forever separate streams.

If this is so, vast new powers may lie within our grasp. By learning to control and direct the sprawling forces of progressive ambiguity, we can attack the unknown with a tactical skill never before possible, extending the boundaries of our comprehension to new and unexplored regions.

CHAPTER 10

Progressive Ambiguity Helps the Growth of Knowledge

The sense growths undergone by words and allied symbols parallel and facilitate the growth of meaning. Creative thinking is largely a matter of making symbols progressively ambiguous, of causing them to assume new tasks according to logical patterns of analysis.

A new meaning is born whenever the mind uses a word or other symbol in a new way. If you think of a key as something to open a lock and then speak of hard work as the key to success, you are using the word *key* in a new way. It no longer means simply a metal implement for opening a lock; it has acquired a much richer sense in your mind: "necessary prerequisite for attaining a desired goal." If the word *key* were not free to shift its sense, the new concept probably could not emerge.

All thinkers, whether artists, philosophers, scientists, businessmen, or laborers, can create new thoughts if they use words in new ways. These new uses ordinarily emerge via one or a combination of the six routes previously described.

Poets are notorious "image-makers"; their "metaphors" or "flowers of rhetoric" are simply words transported to new environments for poetic effect, intended to spark new flashes of meaning in the minds of their readers. Walt Whitman, in *Song of Myself*, calls grass "the handkerchief of the Lord." Mark Twain, in *Roughing It*, describes Lake Tahoe, viewed by starlight, as a "great mirror, spangled with jewels."

Ideas, feelings, and beliefs can be expressed with clarity and force by the use of words in contexts where they "don't belong." Transferring *tree* and *manure* to the sphere of politics, Thomas Jefferson (in a letter to a friend) implies a relation between continued freedom and periodic revolution: "The tree of liberty must be refreshed from time to time with the blood of patriots and tyrants. It is its natural manure." John Donne helps us to comprehend our dependence on one another by transplanting words such as *island* and *continent* to a discussion of man's relation to man: "No man is an island, entire of itselfe; every man is a peece of the Continent, a part of the maine; if a clod bee washed away by the Sea, Europe is the lesse, as well as if a Promontorie were . . . any man's death diminishes me, because I am involved in mankinde . . ." Such sentiments simply could not be expressed were language not free to change its colors.

Verbal shifts are by no means limited to literary or abstract subjects. Scientists, engineers, and other "practical" creators often use words in new ways for a very good reason: their innovations, precisely because they have never before existed, have never been named. These new things are usually "lent" names of pre-existing things which are like them in some way. *Bulb,* the name of the spherical bud of a tulip or onion, became the name of Thomas Edison's invention. When clocks were invented, their movable indicators were given the name of a man's five-fingered extremity. When periodical collections of stories, articles, and the like came into being, they were called *magazines*, a name which formerly meant, among other things: a room in a fort or ship for storing gunpowder; a warehouse or depot, especially for the storage of military goods; a chamber in a firearm for holding and feeding cartridges.

This transference of old words to new spheres of inquiry encourages the growth of new concepts. When men sent words such as *ring, bond,* and *family* to the field of chemistry, they created concepts such as the benzene "ring"; the "bond" between atoms causing them to cling together as molecules; the halogen "family" of elements. Newly created senses of old words usually accompany newly created thoughts or objects. "Creativity" is largely a process of making words increasingly ambiguous, of taking them out of their ordinary uses and transporting them to new realms of meaning.

Nonlinguistic symbols, too, encourage the growth of ideas, as they acquire new meanings. For you, an arrow ($\rightarrow$) may originally mean to proceed in a certain direction. If you see an arrow above the word *exit* in a theater, you know that you must "go this way" to get out. If you transfer the arrow to a formula, such as $2H_2 + O_2 \rightarrow 2H_2O$, it acquires a much different meaning in your mind, helping you to think about the "direction" of a chemical reaction. In this new sense, the arrow no longer has to do with change of location in space, but with transformation of substance in time. The chemicals stay in the same place; the $2H_2$ and O_2 do not get up from their seats and walk toward $2H_2O$. The arrow has a new meaning, related to the old one but much different from it; it means that if you place hydrogen and oxygen together, the *result*, after a chemical reaction, will be water.

Diagrams can aid the growth of thought by taking on new symbolic meaning. What does the diagram below signify? Let us assume that it has its original use in a biological classification, in which animals and plants are shown to be types of organisms, and vertebrates and invertebrates are shown to be types of animals. If transferred to the sphere of corporate structure, this diagram can acquire new significance, facilitating thoughts about the hierarchical arrangements of employees. Smith is over Jones and Brown; Jones is over Miller and Fox. Jones and Brown are not *sorts* of Smith, as animals and plants are sorts of organisms.

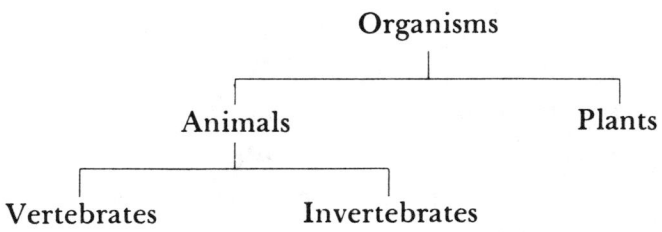

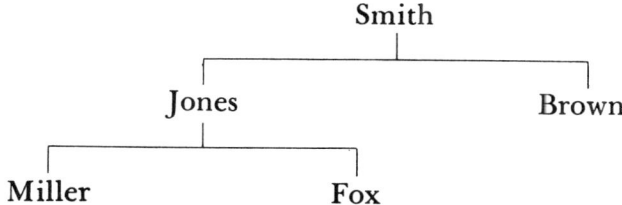

The lines of the diagram now signify levels and directions of authority, rather than sub-classes of a general class.

The diagram can take on numerous other senses, if transferred to other areas. It could, for example, grow to represent the outcomes of decisions. If you stay home, you can watch TV or read; if you watch TV, you can turn on a Western or a quiz show. Used in this new way, indicating clusters of possible decisions,

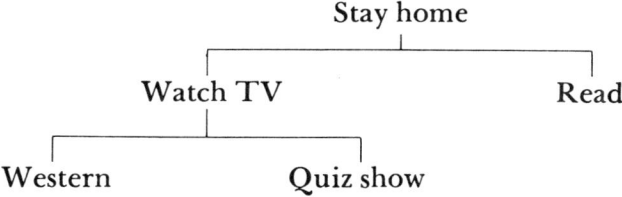

such a diagram might help a military planner chart the best course in a campaign, or a company president determine the most efficient policies in manufacturing and marketing a product.

All charts, graphs, diagrams, and other such representational devices are similarly ambiguous, possessing the power to generate and guide new thoughts as they shift their symbolic functions.

Nonlinguistic symbols of every kind can adapt themselves to new meanings. Because the numerals 0 and 1 could be altered in meaning, binary mathematics (and the computer technology based upon it) was developed. The number 11010 can now mean twenty-six as well as eleven thousand and ten; thus we live in an age of binary computers rather than of decimal adding machines.

Symbols such as +, −, X, A, B, %, and . grow new senses daily, giving form to man's emerging thoughts. Sometimes the new senses grow through arbitrary designation, bearing little or no relation to old senses. An aviation engineer may say, "Let x equal the pitch of an aircraft wing," arbitrarily defining x in a new way, without relation to earlier meanings, such as "the number of men required to lay one hundred yards of track in an hour," or "the deviation of a score from the average."

At other times the new senses grow through meaningful connection with old senses. The symbol + possesses a number of old senses, such as positive, add, in connection with, extra. If placed on a map of the world, the plus sign may take on a new sense which is related to the old ones: North. (South, of course, will be signified by —.) North is up or positive, as opposed to South, which is down or negative. Here is another symbol which has recently grown a new sense seemingly related to its old ones: .. Two of the old senses are period, the end of a sentence; and decimal point, the end of a whole number and the beginning of a fraction. The new sense is "halt," an instruction to an electronic computer to stop its operation until a human operator decides what to do next.

All symbols can grow new meanings if used in new ways, whether they are numbers, diagrams, mathematical signs, words, or what have you. Our minds shift to new thoughts as these symbols shift to new meanings.

Often, perhaps always, words and nonlinguistic symbols cooperate in the growth of concepts, ideas, objects. Consider a pencil line and the word *line*. These two symbols usually perform as a team in helping draftsmen, engineers, and other visual creators perform their work. A man cannot create a three-dimensional object on paper unless he comprehends at least to some degree an abstract sense of the word *line* (or its equivalent). He may create such a sense as follows. He observes that "lines" are objects such as cords, ropes, wires, pencil marks, rows of people, rows of printed words. Thinking about what these objects have in common, he abstracts the quality of "lineness" from them, giving the word *line* a new, abstract sense: "the path of a moving point, having length but no breadth." Having thus freed, with the new sense of the word *line*, the quality of "lineness" from real objects, he is capable of thinking in geometrical terms, manipulating lines with points, angles, surfaces, and solid forms in the invention of buildings, tools, machines.

Now let us consider the "line" such a man might draw with a pencil on a piece of paper. This mark is the symbolic partner of the word *line,* meaning path of a moving point. This line drawn with a pencil is not a "line," for a line has no width, and a trail of graphite certainly does; it is an invisible concept only. This pencil "line" is a symbol. It actually has the same meaning as the word *line*. It represents an invisible length, with no width of its own — for example, the place where two surfaces meet.

An architect may draw pencil "lines" to represent the edges of a building. These marks symbolize "lines" — lengths with no width, places where surfaces meet. But these marks have no automatic meaning by themselves. The word *line,* in its abstract sense, helps define for the architect what the marks mean. Pencil "lines" and the word *line* (together with other verbal and nonverbal symbols) help a complex structure to grow in the architect's mind. Without speech, the meaning of the lines probably could not be comprehended. Unable to use the word *line,* an ape or a dog can never know that marks on paper represent a building.

Our language helps us interpret other symbols. Words and nonlinguistic symbols join hands, shifting to new senses together in the flux of meaning's growth.

Today's civilization is largely the outgrowth of the past growth of symbolic meaning. Words provide the most observable example. History records not only changing events but changing senses of words as well. Common English words, centuries old, have sprouted meanings which Shakespeare never dreamed of. Let us imagine that a man's mind is a motion picture screen on which pictures are flashed in response to words. What differing pictures might the same words produce in the minds of an Englishman of the Elizabethan era and an American today?

The word *train* might cause the sixteenth-century man to visualize such things as the train (trailing part) of a dress; the train (tail feathers) of a peacock; a train of followers in a retinue; or a train of events. The same word might cause the twentieth-century man to visualize these additional things: a train of gears and a train of railroad cars. To the Elizabethan mind, the word *wing* might bring a picture of a bird's wing or a wing of a building. In addition to these, the modern mind might see a picture of the wing of an airplane. The word *cell* might trigger in the Elizabethan mind thoughts of a small monastery connected to a larger one; a small cavity, as in a honeycomb; or a small room, as in a convent, monastery, or prison. On the motion picture screen of the modern mind a picture of a storage battery cell, a cell of living protoplasm, or a Communist Party cell might appear.

The newly created senses of English words would be as unfamiliar to William Shakespeare or Francis Bacon as communications satellites, transistor radios, and psychoanalysis. A hood, in addition to being a portion of a garment, is now part of an automobile. Airplanes, as well as men and animals, have noses. Photographic negatives and prints, as well as people, are immersed in baths. Islands exist not only in oceans but in highways. Typewriters and examinations, as well as locks, have keys. Ghosts appear on television screens as well as in castles. A jet is not only a stream of liquid or gas, but also an airplane. The new senses of our words reflect the progress of our society.

The process never stops. As a particular science grows new concepts, words grow new meanings, because concepts are simply the result of certain sorts of words at work. In the advancement of electronic computer technology, old English words have acquired (and will continue to acquire) strange new senses. *Memory* now means not only the mind's capacity for storing past experiences, but also a computer's net-like cube for retaining electronic symbols. *Read* and *write* have grown to mean something more than what a person does with his eyes and hand: computers "read" holes punched in cards; they "write" words and numbers on "printing units" and whirling "disks." *Program* now means not only something presented on the stage, or on a radio or television set; it means something in a computer — a series of "instructions" which the computer "executes." The word *address,* meaning where a person or institution resides, has sprouted the new sense "location in memory where a unit of information may be found." The word *word* itself has acquired a new sense in computer technology. A "word" is one or more numeric and/or alphabetic characters or "bits" in a computer's memory. This, for example, may be a word: A934H5T.

Examples of sense growth can be found in every discipline which has undergone change. As airplanes grew wings and tails, *wing* and *tail* grew new senses. *Chain* came to mean something more than a series of metal links when physicists discovered and created chain reactions. When the first Earth satellite went into orbit, the word *satellite* became the name of a man-made object as well as a natural one, such as the moon or Venus. As our world changes, our language changes too. In fact, changes in our language help us to conceive and subsequently to effect changes in our world.

As men invent new objects or concepts, they usually invent new meanings for words and other symbols as part of the same operation.

It is intriguing to think of the role of symbolic sense growth in the unwritten history of the future. What new meanings will words, numbers, diagrams, mathematical signs, and the other members of the symbolic family acquire as we extend our knowledge of the universe? What exotic new colors will they take on as we send them to unexplored regions? Surely these new meanings will be as strange to us as the concepts of an atomic mushroom and a magnetic field would have been to Shakespeare, who knew only vegetable mushrooms and earthly fields.

One fact seems apparent. We can accelerate the progress of knowledge by becoming more aware of the way new knowledge grows, through the adapting of words and other symbols to new functions. We must understand that words are like the god Proteus, who had great but elusive powers. When the other gods sought him out for his gift of prophecy, he would elude them by changing his shape. Words will become our dependable servants only when we learn their protean secret of systematic change. Keenly aware of this natural symbolic flux, we can control it with heightened skill. Perhaps we can, in a sense, evolve a higher mind, a captain of a functioning but unruly crew. Integrating diverse and haphazard mental forces, this "overmind" can guide us with a clearer view and greater speed toward whatever horizon we may choose.

CHAPTER 11

Toward a New Mental Plateau?

By improving our use of words, we may transform the quality of our thought. Dr. Upton's methods, if widely applied, might boost the American intellect to new heights. If the improvement mirrored by a ten-point increase in IQ scores can be brought about during a single year of schooling, what vastly greater improvement might be achieved during eight or twelve years?

Perhaps, on the heels of the "new mathematics" revolution, we shall embark upon a parallel revolution in language instruction. This will be a radical departure from present practices, which stress the communicative and artistic uses of words, to the neglect of the problem-solving function. Students are taught grammar, composition, creative writing, and English literature — subjects which (as conventionally taught) have too little to do with the logical processes of thought. Seldom are students given formal, rigorous training in definition, classification, and the other problem-solving functions. The perfunctory training in "outlining" is a far cry from the demanding discipline of operation analysis.

Systematic theory and training may produce exciting results. How differently might a new generation of Americans think, if trained from kindergarten through graduate school in this neglected area? If words play the vital part in our thinking that Professor Upton's experiment indicates, we might achieve an unparalleled level of brilliance — a level formerly reserved for the rare genius, the Einstein or Edison.

Perhaps all of us, by learning to use words more skillfully, can elevate our analytic ability and transform our view of the world. The exercises in this book may provide a first step toward these dramatic mental changes.

EXERCISES

Directions

Necessitating a systematic use of words and other mental symbols, the exercises are intended to improve your ability to solve practical problems of all kinds, whether in science, the arts, business, or your personal life. Though they are artificial and "made up," these problems demand the same mental processes as do the problems of the real world. If you can solve the most difficult exercises in this book, you can probably solve many of the most difficult problems in life, provided you are sufficiently persistent.

The exercises are divided into seven levels, according to difficulty, from "Very Easy" to "Very Difficult." Each level is composed of a mixture of problems emphasizing the use of words in thing-making, qualification, classification, structure analysis, operation analysis, and analogy.

At some point, perhaps midway between Level 1 and Level 7, you may find that the exercises have become too difficult for you. Do not give up; this is the very point at which you can make real progress. Just as a weight lifter builds his muscles by progressively lighting weights which are a trifle "too heavy" for him, so you can improve your powers of analysis by persistently solving problems which are a little harder than ones you have solved before. If you are able to work your way through Level 6 or Level 7, you will have demonstrated a very high degree of mental ability.

Each exercise has its own directions. The answers begin on page 183.

LEVEL I

Very Easy

1. Which item (a, b, c, or d) is the opposite of the one at left?

2. Which object (a, b, or c) belongs with the two at left?

3. Which item (a, b, c, or d) is the same as the one at left?

4. Which drawing (a, b, or c) goes in the blank space?

5. Which item (a, b, c, or d) is the same as the one at left?

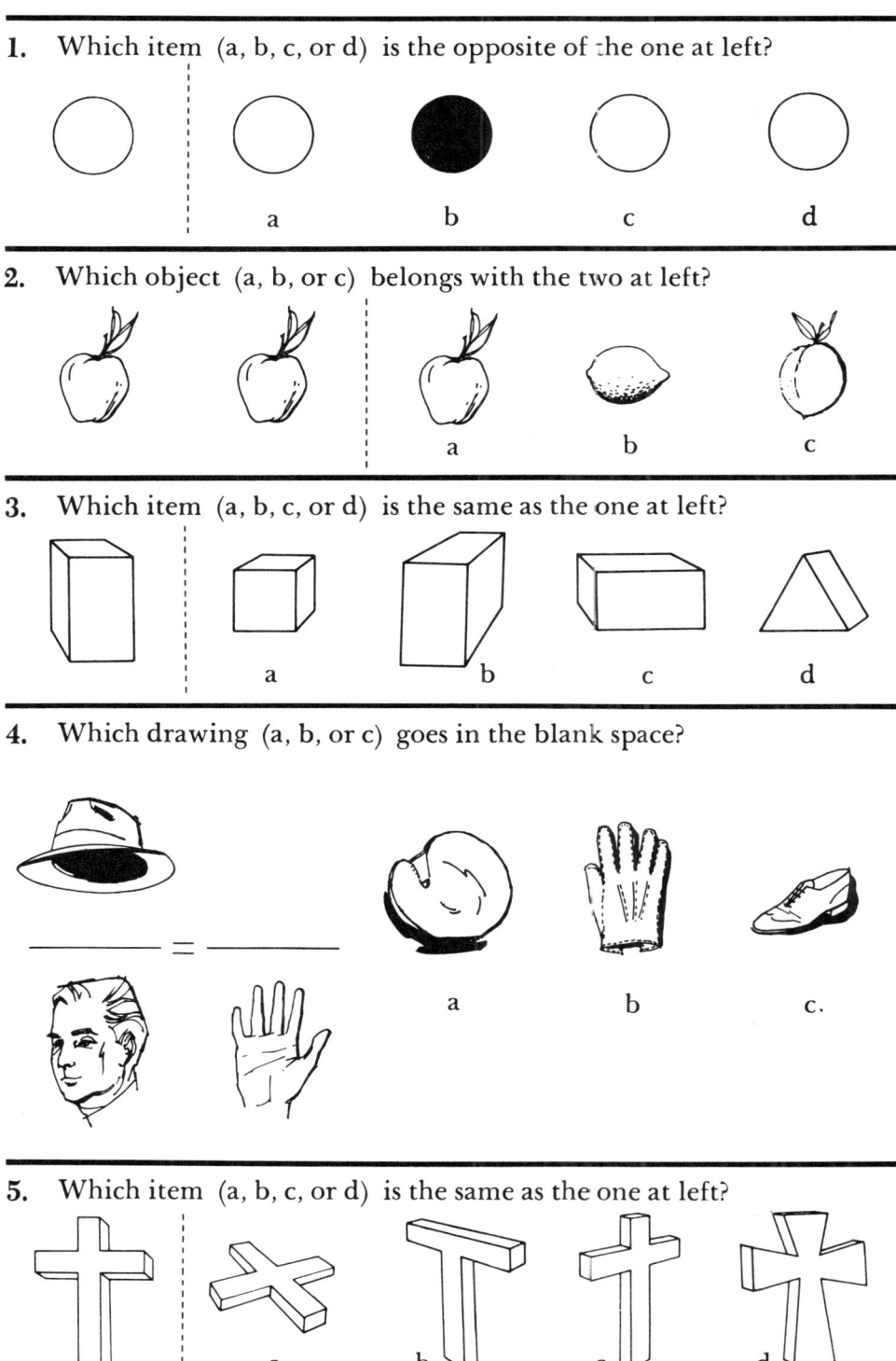

6. Which item (a, b, or c) belongs with the two at left?

    a   b   c

7. Which item (a, b, or c) belongs in the blank space?

SWEET

—— = ——   SOUR   YELLOW

     a   b   c

8. Which item (a, b, c, or d) is the opposite of the one at left?

     a   b   c   d

9. Which drawing (a, b, c, or d) comes next in the sequence?

1   2   3   4   5

a   b   c   d

10. Which answer choice (a, b, or c) goes in the blank space?

OXXOXXOXX_____OXXOXX   OXX   OXO   XXO

                                                  a   b   c

11. Which drawing (a, b, or c) goes in the blank space?

12. Which drawing (a, b, c, or d) is the same as the one at left?

13. Match each use of the word *comb* with the proper meaning, at right.

| She has a lovely *comb* in her hair. | A | a |
| That's a rooster; it has a *comb*. | B | b |

14. Which figure (a, b, or c) belongs with the two at left?

    a   b   c

15. Which object (a, b, c, or d) is the opposite of the one at left?

    a   b   c   d

16. What number comes next in the sequence?

    19, 17, 15, 13, 11, 9, 7, _____

17. Which item (a, b, c, or d) is the same as the one at left?

    a   b   c   d

18. Which drawing (a, b, or c) belongs with the two at left?

    a   b   c

19. Which answer choice (a, b, or c) belongs in the blank space of the sequence?

    AAaaBBb_____Ccc   bB   cC   bC

                            a   b   c

20. Which drawing (a, b, c, or d) is the opposite of the one at left?

a b c d

21. Which drawing (a, b, c, or d) is the same as the one at left?

a b c d

22. Which drawing (a, b, c, or d) is the same as the one at left?

a b c d

23. Pick the answer choice (a, b, or c) which belongs in the blank space.

a b c

24. Which word (a, b, c, or d) belongs in the blank space of the series?

SECOND, MINUTE, HOUR, DAY, _____, MONTH

| WEEK | YEAR | SATURDAY | NIGHT |
| a | b | c | d |

25. Pick the word (a, b, c, or d) which is the opposite of the first.

BIRTH	CHILDHOOD	DEATH	INFANT	ADULTHOOD
	a	b	c	d

26. Pick the drawing (a, b, or c) which best completes the analogy.

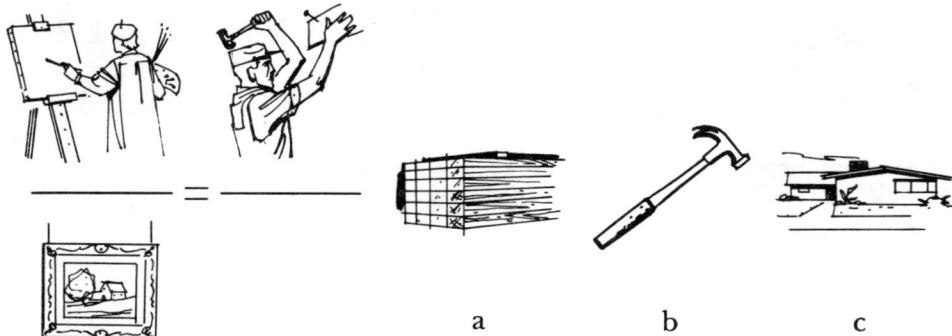

27. Which drawing (a, b, or c) belongs with the two on the left?

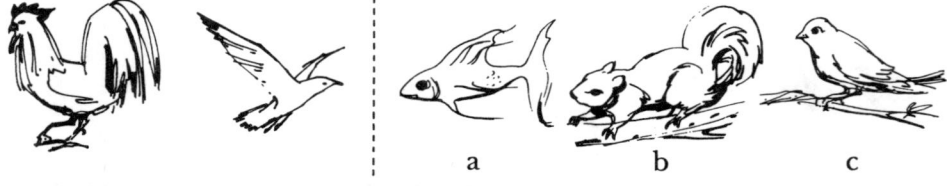

28. Match each use of the word *baseball* with the corresponding meaning, at right.

| John got a new *baseball* for Christmas. | A | a |  |
| I enjoy *baseball* more than football. | B | b |  |

LEVEL 2
Easy

1. Which drawing (a, b, c, or d) is the same as the one at left?

   a   b   c   d

2. Pick the word (a, b, c, or d) which is opposite the first.

   RED   GREEN   BLUE   YELLOW   ORANGE
           a   b   c   d

3. Which drawing (a, b, or c) belongs with the two on the left?

   a   b   c

4. Choose the object (a, b, or c) which completes the analogy.

   ___ = ___

   a   b   c

5. Pick the answer choice (a, b, or c) which goes in the blank space of the sequence.

   121212ABABAB1212_____BAB   12ABC   12ABA   ABABA
                                   a   b   c

6. Pick the object (a, b, or c) which is most similar to the two at left.

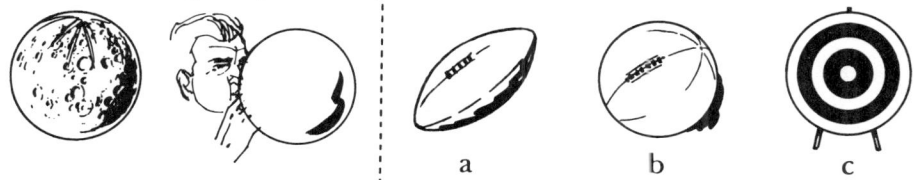

7. Think of at least three different meanings of the word *letter*.

8. Which drawing (a, b, c, or d) is the same as the one at left?

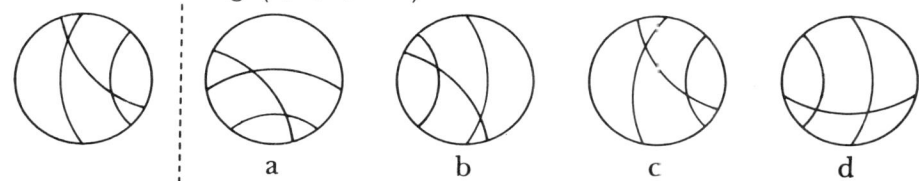

9. Which item (a, b, or c) completes the analogy? Why?

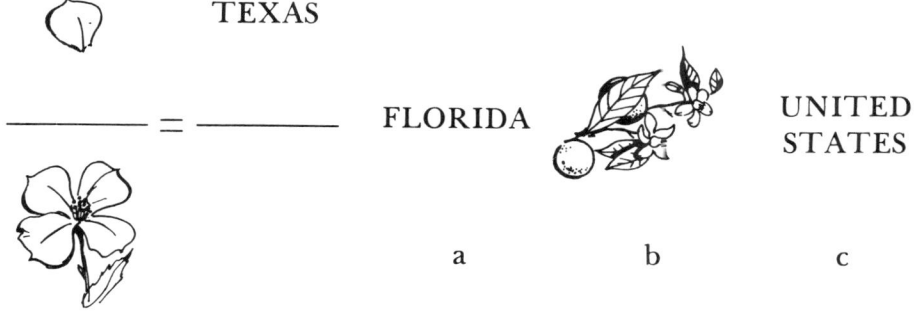

10. Which drawing (a, b, c, or d) is the opposite of the one at left?

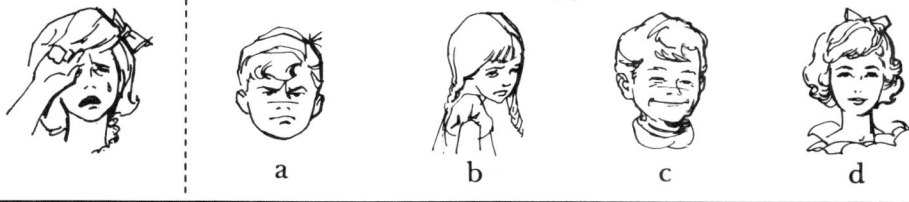

11. At random, name five or ten qualities which these drawings call to mind. For example: BROKEN, MOVING, HANGING.

    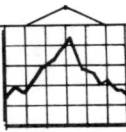

12. Which answer choice (a, b, or c) completes the analogy?

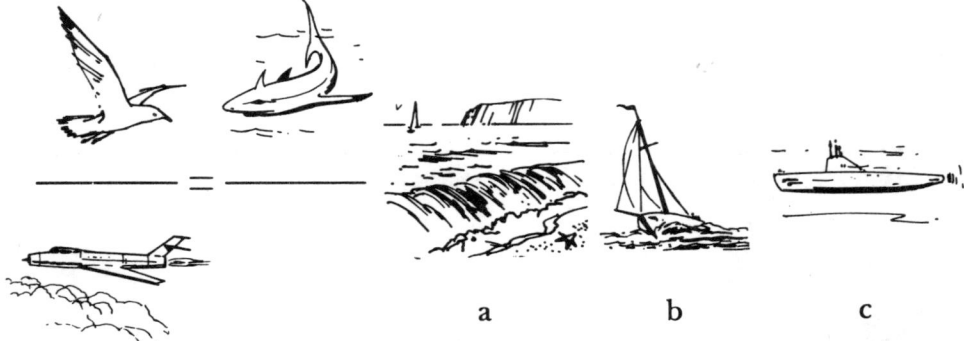

a   b   c

13. What object (a, b, c, or d) is the same as the one at left?

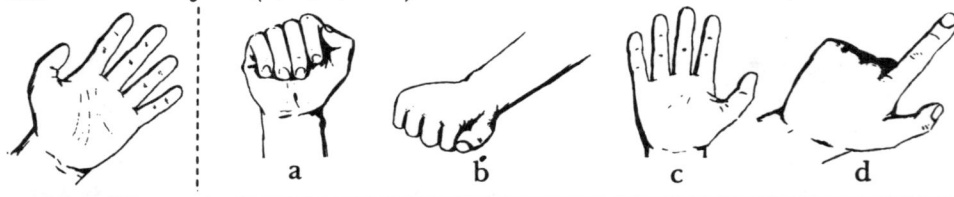

a   b   c   d

14. Match each use of the word *radiant* with the corresponding meaning, indicated at right.

"Sorrow for the lost Lenore— For the rare and *radiant* maiden whom the angels name Lenore— Nameless here for evermore." Edgar Allan Poe, *The Raven*	A a	 Showing happiness, joy
Like a *radiant* star, his soul shone with a brilliance of its own, cold, distant, pure white.	B b	 Shining brightly

15. Which set of letters (a, b, or c) belongs in the blank space of the series?

123454321ABCD_____BA	EDC	C	EC
	a	b	c

16. How does the meaning of *ring* shift, from the first sentence to the second?   With this *ring* I thee wed.
    Through the telescope he saw Saturn's *ring*.
    (a) by structure analysis (whole to part),   (b) by thing-making (thing to similar thing),   (c) by operation analysis (stage to operation)

17. Which object (a, b, or c) belongs with the two at left?

18. Which drawing (a, b, c, or d) is the opposite of the one at left?

19. Which item (a, b, c, or d) is the same as the one at left?

20. Which object (a, b, or c) belongs with the two at left?

21. Which answer choice (a, b, or c) completes the sequence?

XOXOXXOXXOXOXOXXOXXOXOXOXXO____

          XOX   XXO   OXO

           a   b   c

22. Which drawing (a, b, or c) belongs in the blank space?

23. What do the lines at right represent? Can you make an object "pop" into view?

24. Which circles go in which boxes? One circle has already been correctly pigeonholed.

25. Which object (a, b, or c) belongs with the two at left?

a	b	c

26. Which word (a, b, or c) completes the analogy?

MORNING / [baby] = DAY / EVENING / NIGHT [old man]
                  a   b   c

27. Pick the word (a, b, c, or d) which is the opposite of the first.

LOVE | AFFECTION   HATE   RAPPORT   FRIENDSHIP
            a   b   c   d

28. Match each use of the word *roar* with the proper meaning, at right.

A. "She will start from her slumber
When gusts shake the door;
She will hear the winds howling,
Will hear the waves *roar*."
    Matthew Arnold,
    The Forsaken Merman

a. Rumbling utterance, as of a bull or lion.

B. ". . . like the *roar* of some pain'd desert lion . . ."
    Matthew Arnold,
    Sohrab and Rustum

b. Loud, deep sound, as of the surf or an engine.

29. Which words go in which spaces of the diagram?

    Blade

    Knife

    Handle

---

30. Which drawing (a, b, c, or d) is the opposite of the first drawing?

    a   b   c   d

---

31. Which line (a, b, or c) best completes the poem? Why?

One, two, three
What do you see?
Four, five, six

a. Tom Mix
b. The river Styx
c. Pipers three

---

32. Which object (a, b, or c) belongs in the same class with the two at left?

    a   b   c

---

33. Which word (a, b, c, or d) best completes the sentence, in your opinion? There is no "right" answer; pick the word which seems best to you.

Poverty and hatred are _____ of war.

(a) roots   (b) leaves   (c) seeds   (d) fruits

---

34. White squares eat more than white circles. Black squares eat more than white squares. Black squares eat less than black circles. Which would make the most economical pet?

Rover   Minerva   Pogo   Snoopy

35. Can you make up a phrase to replace the question mark?

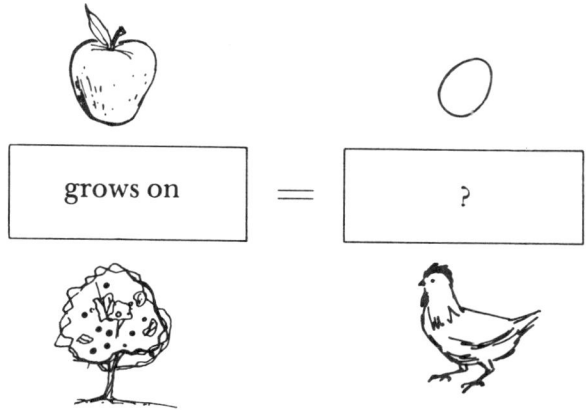

36. Which object (a, b, c, or d) is the opposite of the first object?

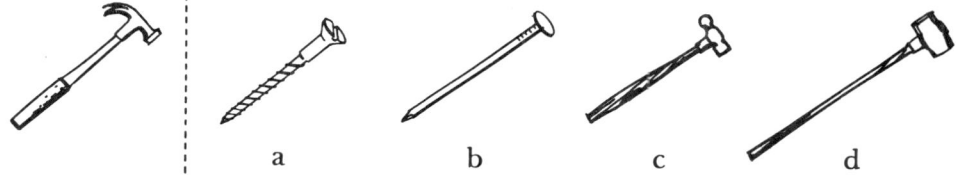

37. Match each use of *jet* with the correct meaning, at right.

The *jet* made a crash landing.	A	a	Stream of gas.
She was an oriental figurine: emerald eyes, ivory skin, *jet* hair.	B	b	Lustrous black.
Increasing its force, the hot *jet* lifted dust, bits of paper, and small pebbles from the runway.	C	c	Airplane which is jet-propelled.

LEVEL 3
Easy−Medium

1. Which object (a, b, or c) belongs in the same class with the two at left?

   a   b   c

2. Which word (a, b, c, or d) is the opposite of the first?

OPPOSITE	SAME	DIFFERENT	QUALITY	ABSTRACT
	a	b	c	d

3. Which answer choice (a, b, or c) goes in the blank space? Try dividing the sequence into "stages," treating it as if it were an operation.

   ABACAABACAABACAABA_____   AB   CA   CB

                                a   b   c

4. Which drawing (a, b, or c) completes the analogy?

   TITIKAKA   ORANA

   ——— = ———

   a   b   c

5. Which object (a, b, c, or d) is the same as the one at left?

   a   b   c   d

6. Think of at least three different meanings of the word *story*.

7. Which item (a, b, or c) goes in the blank space of the analogy?

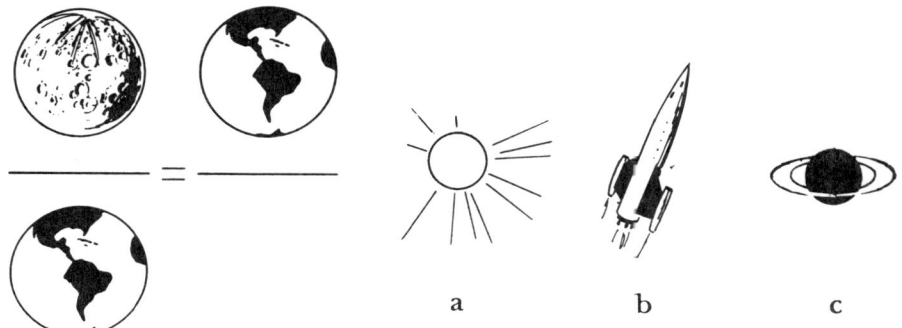

8. Which drawing (a, b, c, or d) is the opposite of the first? Why?

9. Which pictures go in which boxes? Can you think of adequate words to replace the question marks?

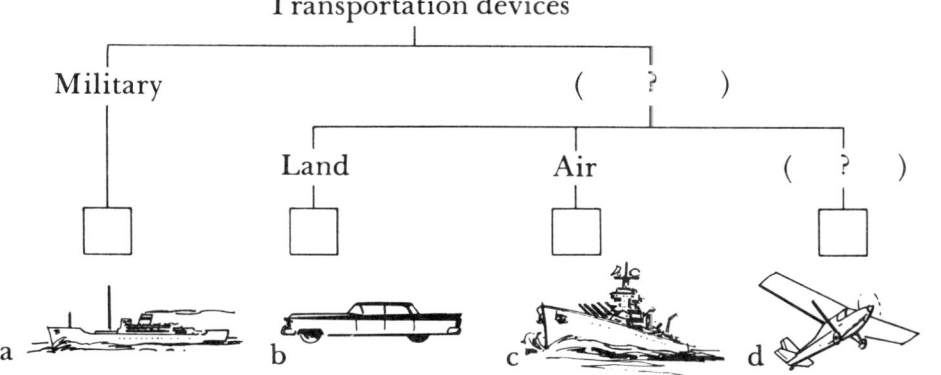

10. Can you make up two different phrases to replace the two question marks?

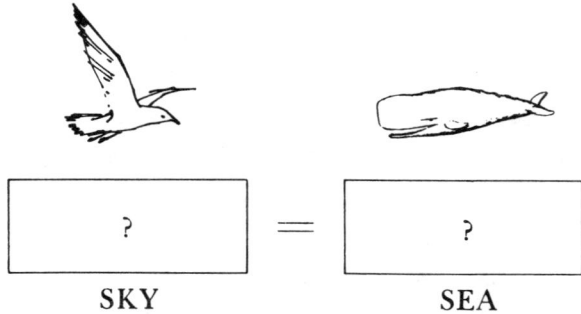

11. Albert is heavier than Bob by a certain amount. Carl is heavier than Dave by the same amount plus ten pounds. Albert is ten pounds heavier than Carl. If Albert weighs 180 pounds and Dave weighs 130 pounds, what is the weight of Bob? The answer is very important to Bob, who fears he may be overweight.

12. Which answer choice (a, b, c, or d) goes in the blank space of the sequence?

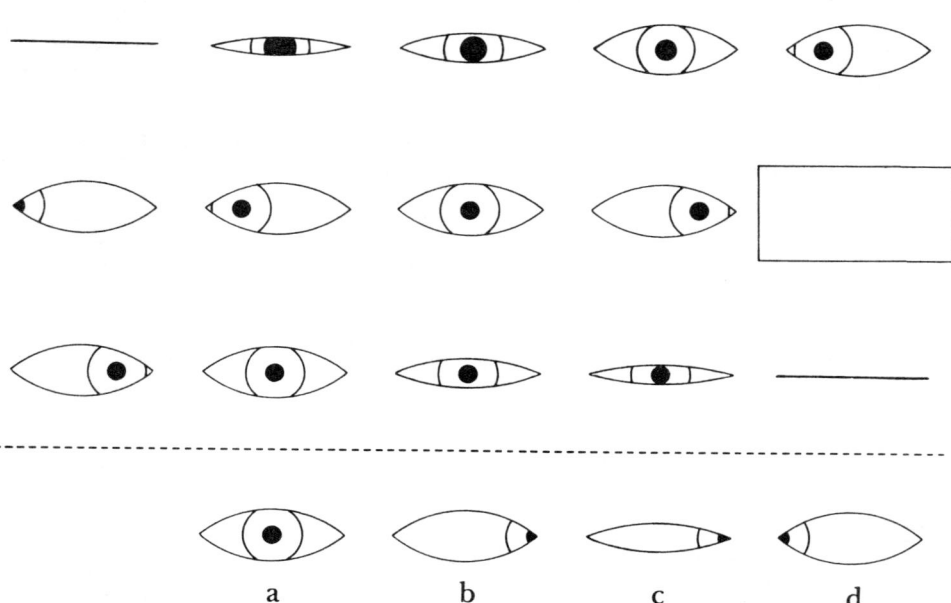

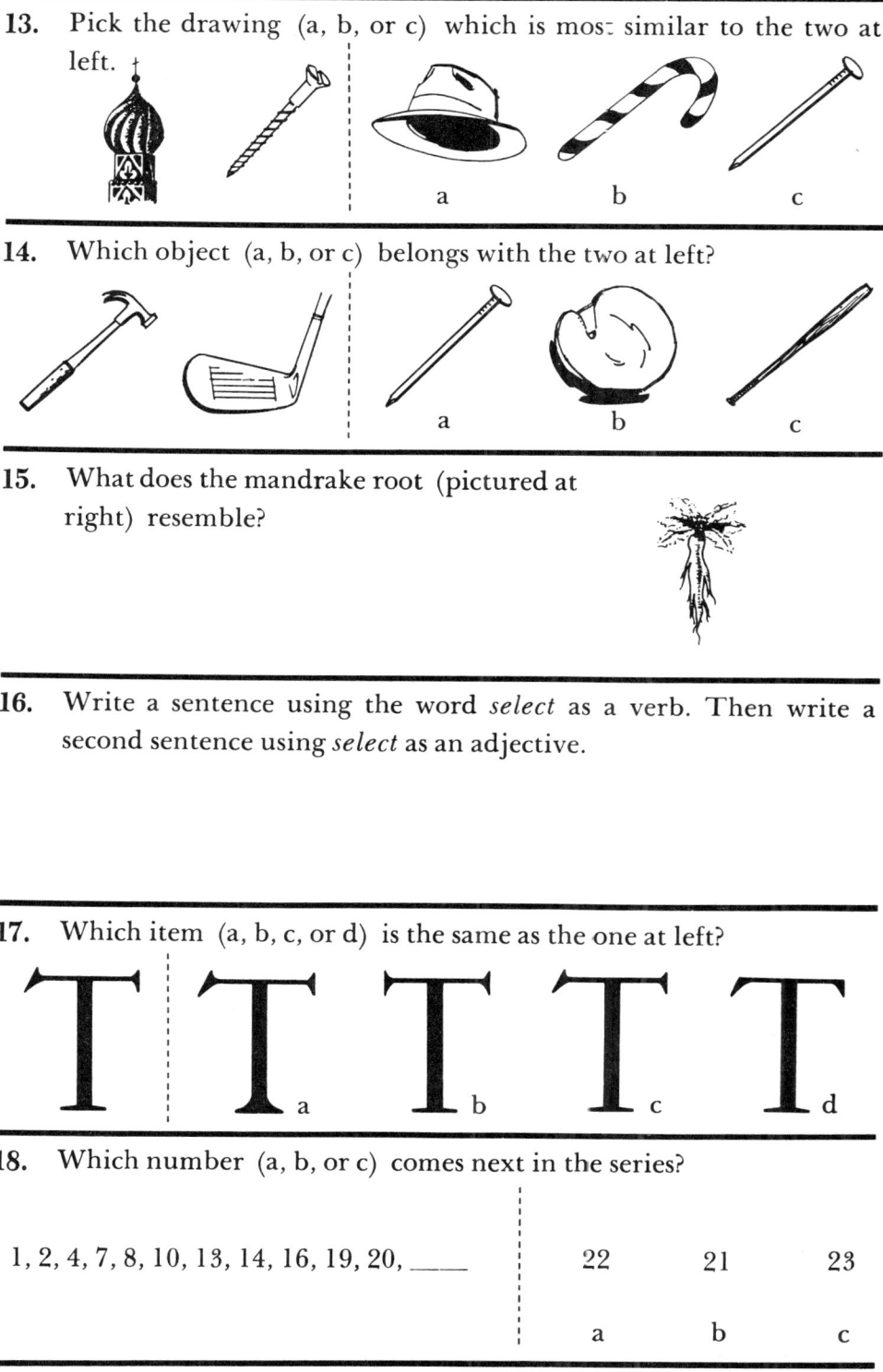

13. Pick the drawing (a, b, or c) which is most similar to the two at left.

    a   b   c

14. Which object (a, b, or c) belongs with the two at left?

    a   b   c

15. What does the mandrake root (pictured at right) resemble?

16. Write a sentence using the word *select* as a verb. Then write a second sentence using *select* as an adjective.

17. Which item (a, b, c, or d) is the same as the one at left?

    a   b   c   d

18. Which number (a, b, or c) comes next in the series?

    1, 2, 4, 7, 8, 10, 13, 14, 16, 19, 20, ___   22   21   23

                                                                                      a   b   c

19. If you were to classify the items below, what sorting factors (names of similar and different qualities) might you consider? Freely name any qualities which come to mind, continuing this list:
ADULT, AGE, BORED, _____, _____, _____, . . .

20. Which answer choice (a, b, or c) goes in the same class with the two objects at left?

21. Which pictures go in which boxes? Can you make up appropriate sorting factors to replace the question marks?

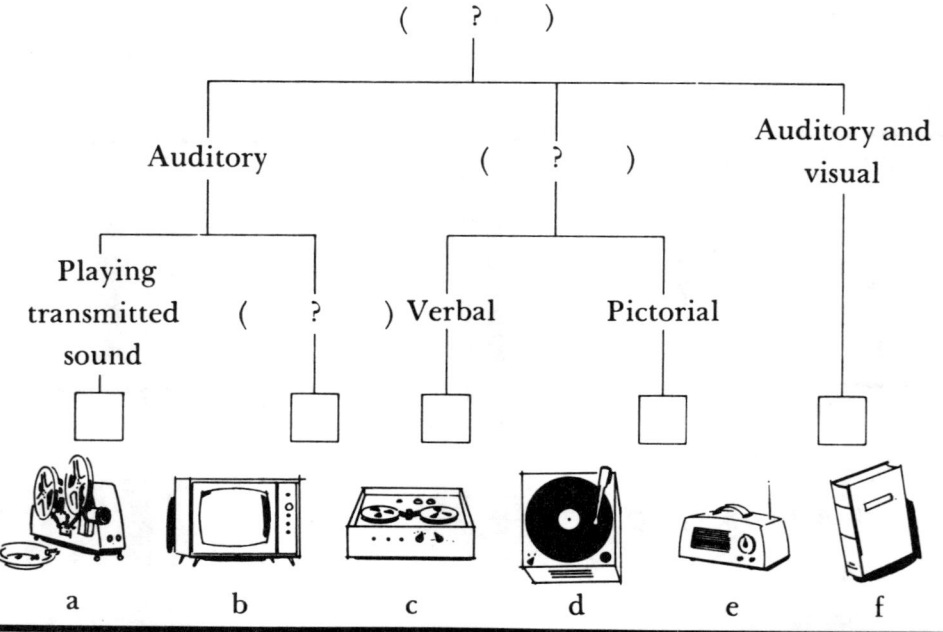

22. Pick the letter (a, b, c, or d) which is the opposite of the first letter.

B	a	D	E	Z
	a	b	c	d

23. Pick the drawing (a, b, or c) which best completes the analogy.

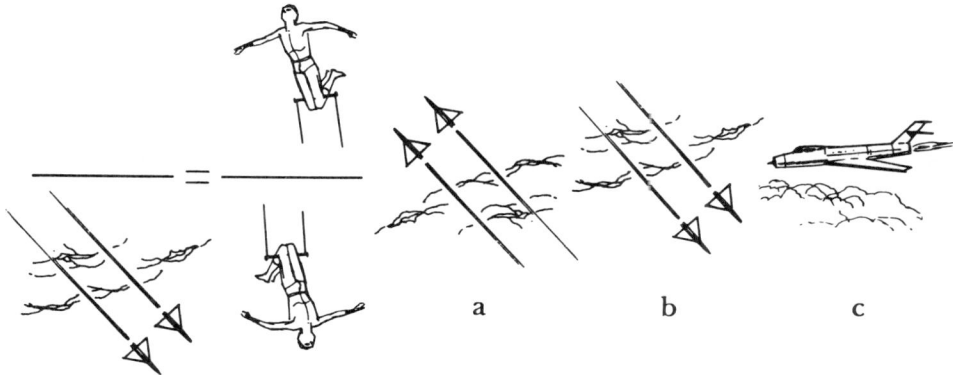

24. How does the meaning of *fish* shift, from the first sentence to the second?

A whale is a mammal, not a *fish*.
A whale is an air-breathing *fish*.

(a) by operation analysis (part to operation), (b) by classification (species to genus), (c) by structure analysis (part to whole)

25. Which answer choice (a, b, c, or d) comes next in the sequence?

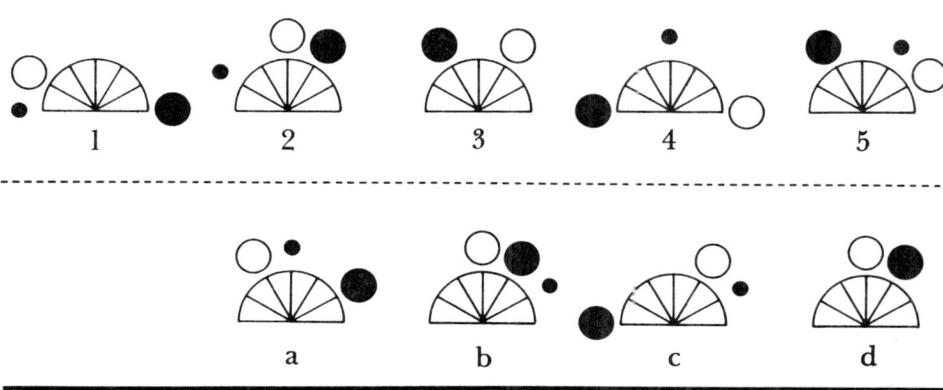

26. Match each use of the word *cat* with the corresponding meaning, indicated at right.

A tiger is a large, fierce *cat* with a striped coat.	A a	
"When I play with my *cat*, who knows whether I do not make her more sport than she makes me?" Michel Montaigne, *Essais*	B b	

27. Which drawing (a, b, or c) belongs with the two at left?

  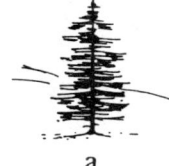  

                                     a   b   c

28. Classify the people at right according to emotional expression and sex, making use of a two-level diagram. For example, books (below) are classified according to size and color. This exercise has no other purpose than the practice it gives in classification.

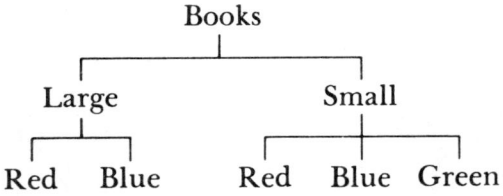

29. Can you make up a phrase to replace the question mark? This phrase should include and be more general than the other two phrases. For example, *child speaks* includes and is more general than *girl whispers* and *boy shouts*.

| is shot by | ? | is hit by |

30. Which object (a, b, c, or d) is the opposite of the first?

a   b   c   d

31. Match each use of *cog* with the appropriate meaning, at right.

The eighth *cog* is broken.	A	a
There are twenty-four teeth on this *cog*.	B	b
Too often, the bright college graduate becomes a mere *cog* in the machinery of business.	C	c

32. How does the meaning of *ocean* shift, from the first sentence to the second?   The *ocean* covers more than two-thirds of Earth's surface. Which *ocean* is larger, the Atlantic or the Pacific?

(a) by operation analysis (stage to operation), (b) by structure analysis (whole to part), (c) by classification (genus to species)

33. Which square (a, b, or c) goes in the blank space of the analogy?

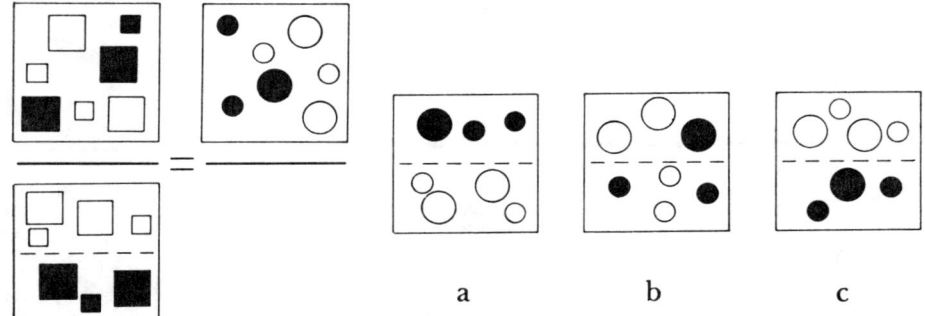

34. Which item (a, b, c, or d) is the same as the one at left?

35. This exercise gives practice in how to divide operations into stages. Rearrange the terms given in the columns at left, placing them in the proper order, at right. The result should be an outline of the sequence of circles.

Growing larger	Growing darker
Changing in shade	Growing lighter
Changing circle	Changing in size
Growing smaller	

36. Can you make up appropriate terms for the blank spaces of the outline?

A. ─────────────

B. ─────────────

  Sorting blacks into
  1. large, medium, small
  2. ─────────────

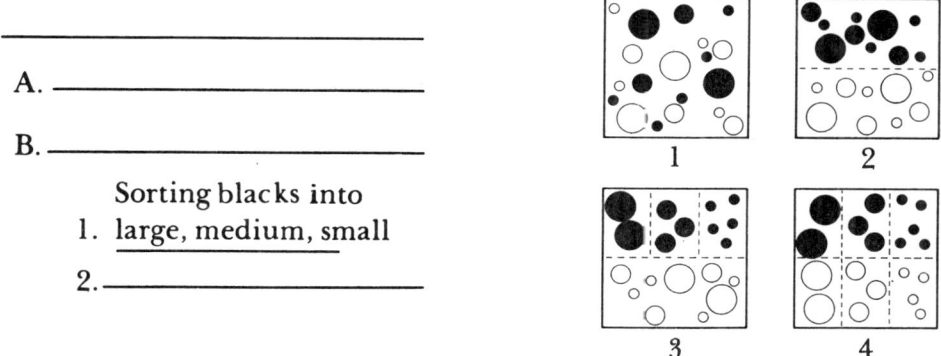

37. Which object (a, b, or c) belongs in the same class with the two at left?

38. Make a classification diagram of the circles below. For example, if you were to classify men, you might make a diagram such as the one shown.

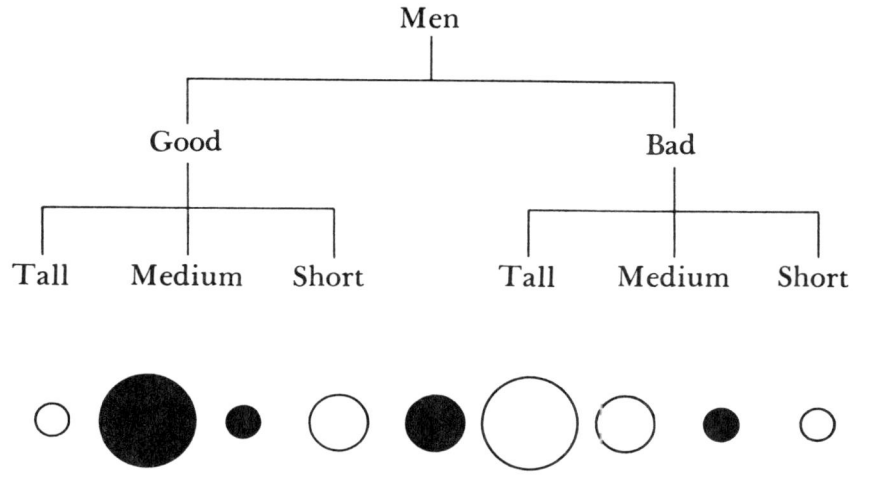

39. Which answer choice (a, b, c, or d) best completes the sentence, in your opinion?

Necessity is the _____ of invention.

(a) parent (b) root (c) hunger pang (d) tinker toy

40. Which word completes the analogy?

$$\frac{\text{BIRTH}}{\text{LIFE}} = \frac{\quad\quad}{\text{DAY}}$$

MORNING	WEEK	SUNRISE
a	b	c

41. Which item (a, b, or c) belongs with the two at left?

42. Which answer choice (a, b, c, or d) best completes the sentence, in your opinion?

Wars between nations are _____ of individual hatreds among individual men.

(a) pyramids built from the stones, (b) composite echoes
(c) fabrics woven from strands, (d) colliding ships blown by the winds

43. How does the meaning of *mushroom* shift, from the first sentence to the second?

Is that a poisonous *mushroom*?
An atomic *mushroom* does not always accompany a nuclear explosion.

(a) by thing-making (thing to similar thing), (b) by qualification (thing to quality), (c) by structure analysis (part to whole)

44. Pick the answer choice (a, b, or c) which best completes the analogy.

$$\frac{\text{ELECTRON}}{\text{ATOM}} = \frac{\text{PLANET}}{\quad\quad}$$

EARTH	SUN	SOLAR SYSTEM
a	b	c

45. If you were a manufacturer of electric light bulbs, how might this incomplete analogy be of value to you?

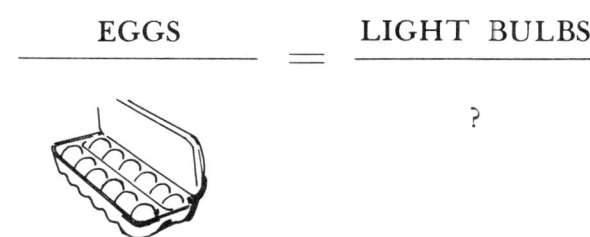

EGGS = LIGHT BULBS

?

46. Which words go in which spaces of the structure analysis diagram? Take the words from the drawing at right.

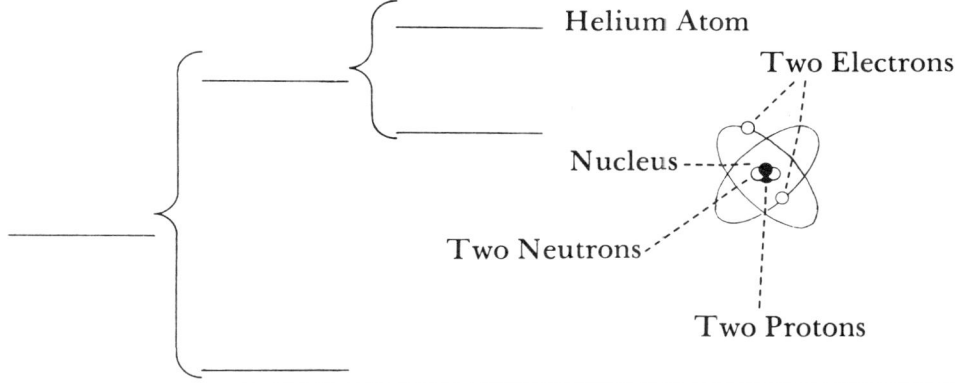

47. What idea does this incomplete analogy give you? What might you invent, thinking in this manner?

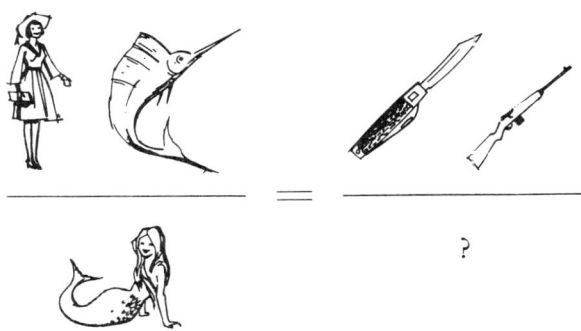

LEVEL 4
Medium

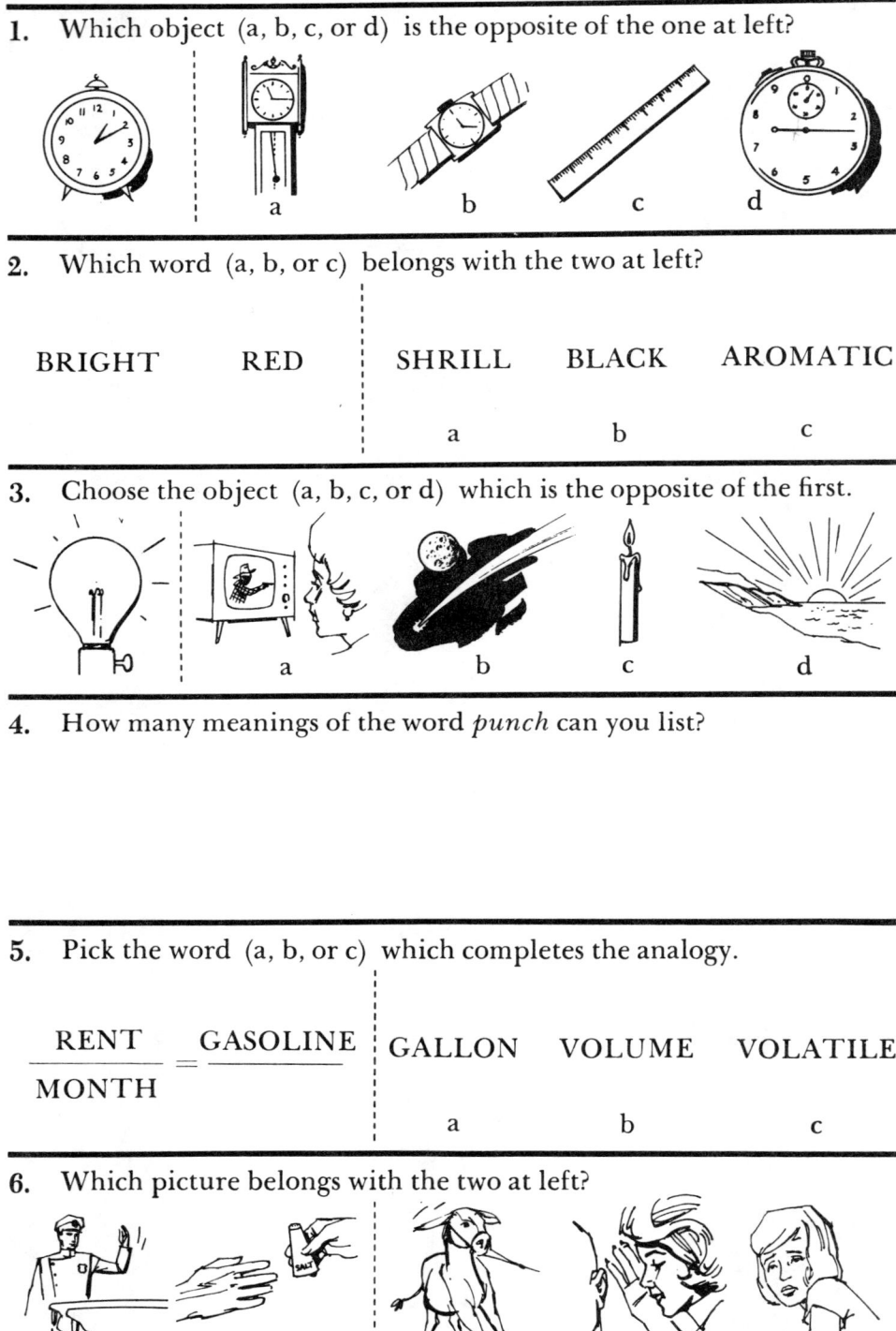

1. Which object (a, b, c, or d) is the opposite of the one at left?

2. Which word (a, b, or c) belongs with the two at left?

   BRIGHT   RED   SHRILL   BLACK   AROMATIC
                    a   b   c

3. Choose the object (a, b, c, or d) which is the opposite of the first.

4. How many meanings of the word *punch* can you list?

5. Pick the word (a, b, or c) which completes the analogy.

   $\dfrac{\text{RENT}}{\text{MONTH}} = \dfrac{\text{GASOLINE}}{}$ GALLON   VOLUME   VOLATILE
                                                                    a   b   c

6. Which picture belongs with the two at left?

7. Which answer choice (a, b, c, or d) continues the sequence?

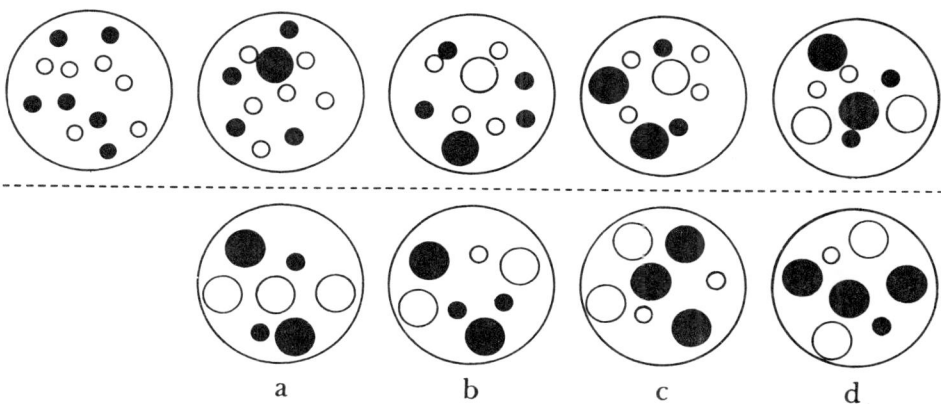

8. Which drawing (a, b, c, or d) is the same as the one at left?

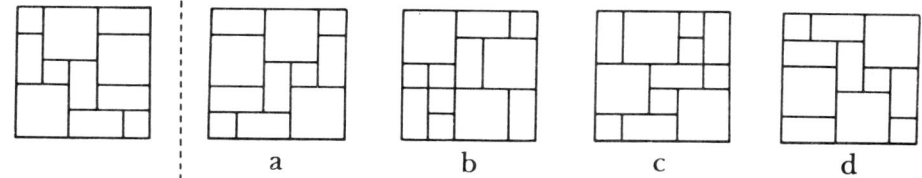

9. The sports illustrated below might be classified in many ways, according to many sorting factors (or named qualities). Add several possible sorting factors to the list which has been started.

INDOOR, OUTDOOR, SEX, MALE, FEMALE, _____, _____, _____, _____, _____, _____, . . .

10. Can you make up two different phrases to replace the two question marks? The phrase in the center box should include and be more general than the phrases in the other two boxes. For example, the phrase *shows irritation* includes and is more general than *swears* and *complains*.

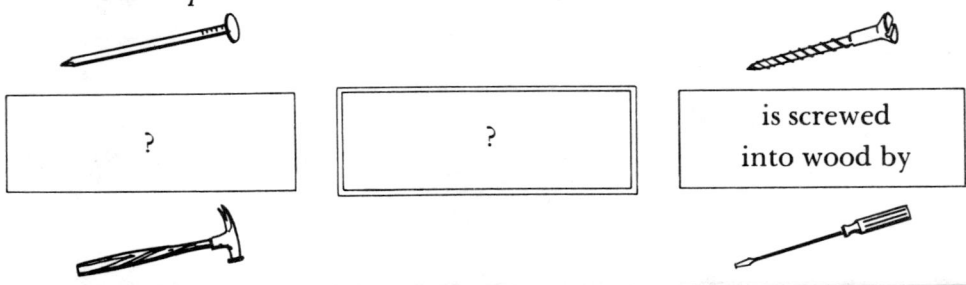

11. Which answer choice (a, b, c, or d) completes the box at left?

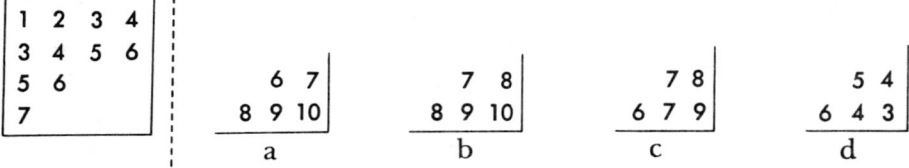

12. Match each use of *tail* with the proper meaning, illustrated at right.

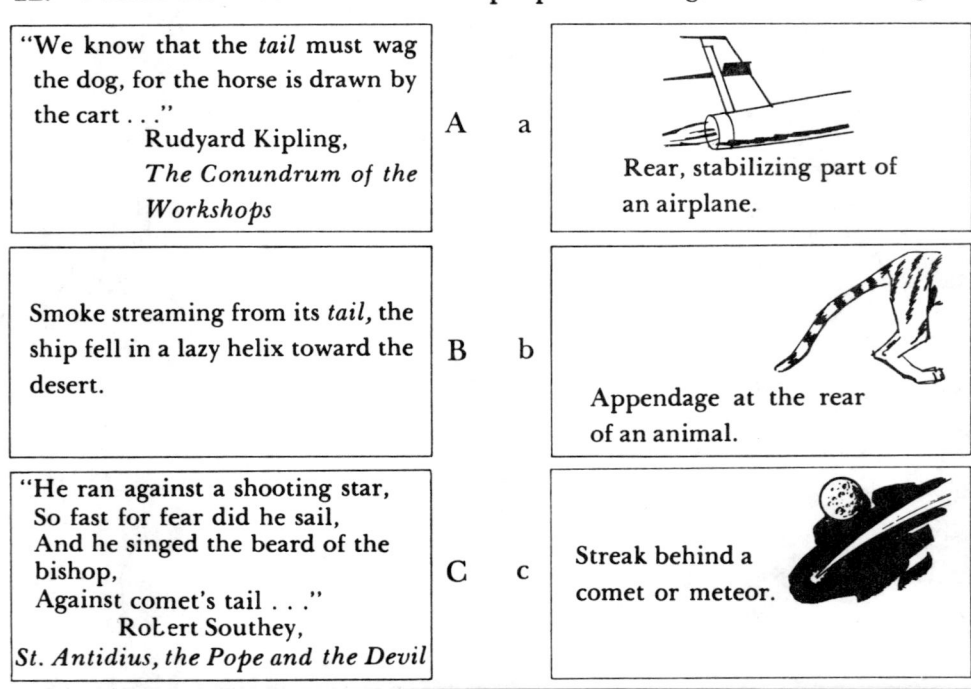

13. Think of at least three meanings of the word *period*.

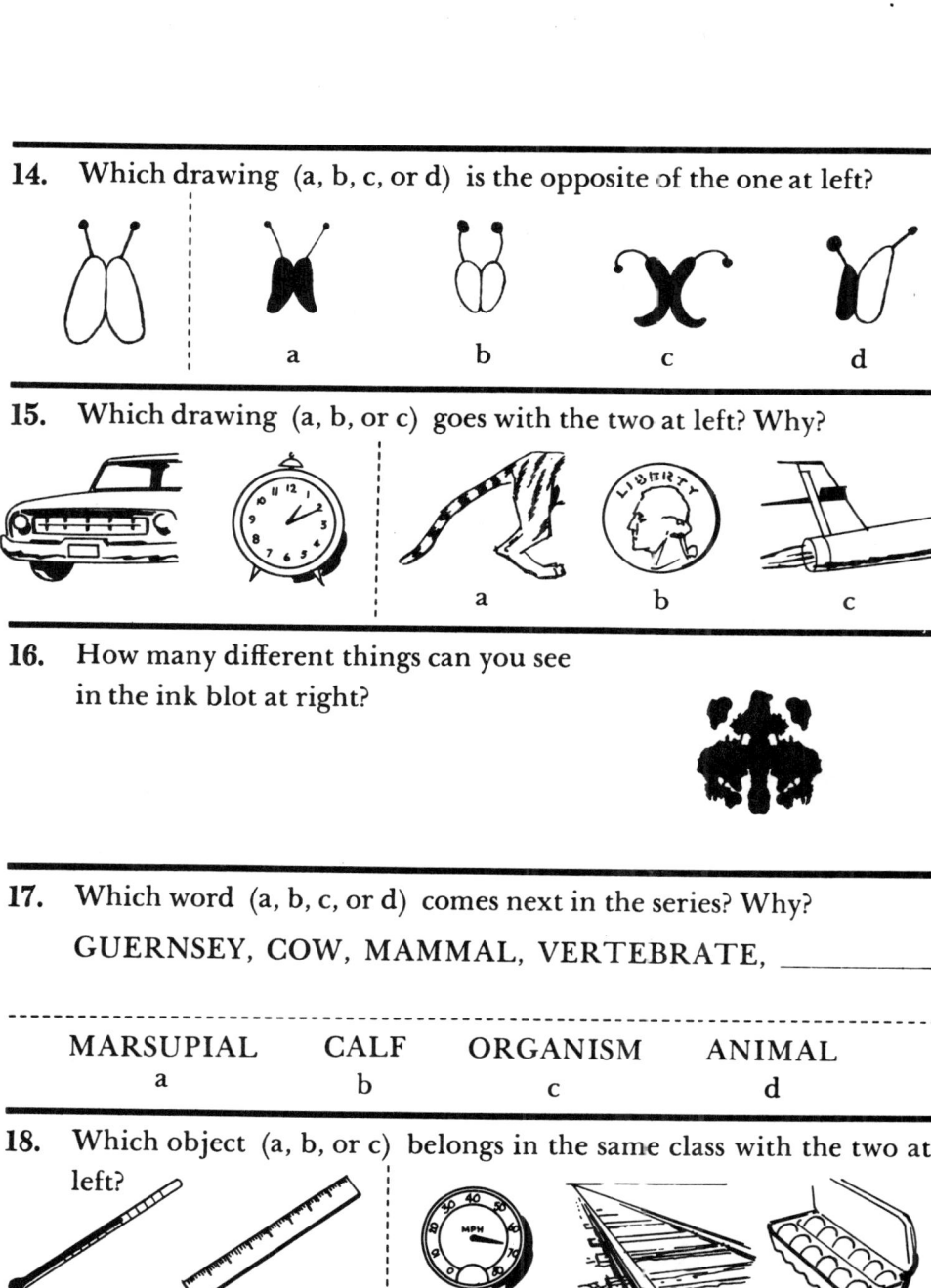

14. Which drawing (a, b, c, or d) is the opposite of the one at left?

    a   b   c   d

15. Which drawing (a, b, or c) goes with the two at left? Why?

    a   b   c

16. How many different things can you see in the ink blot at right?

17. Which word (a, b, c, or d) comes next in the series? Why?
    GUERNSEY, COW, MAMMAL, VERTEBRATE, _____

    MARSUPIAL   CALF   ORGANISM   ANIMAL
        a   b   c   d

18. Which object (a, b, or c) belongs in the same class with the two at left?

    a   b   c

19. Complete the classification diagram begun below. In what ways might the items be classified other than sex and age?

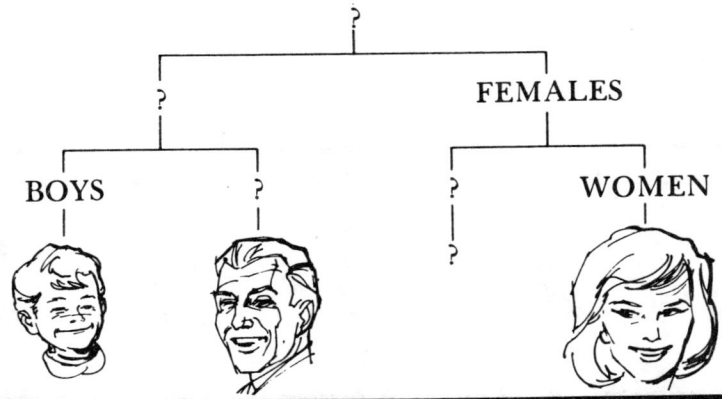

20. Can you make up three different phrases to replace the three question marks? The phrase in the center box should include and be more general than the phrases in the other two boxes. For example, the phrase *animal moves* includes and is more general than *man walks* and *bird swoops*.

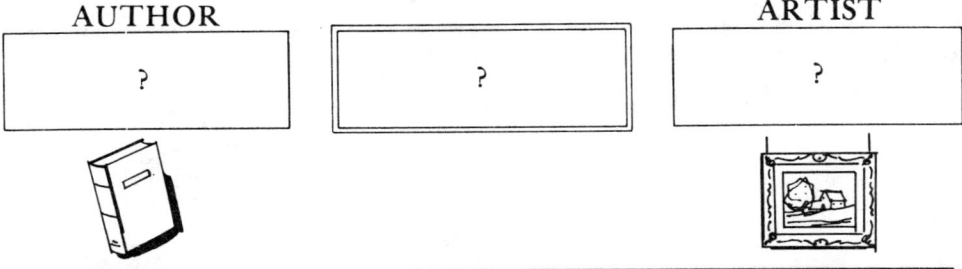

21. Town X is east of town Y. Town Y is east of town Z. Tom, who lives in town X, has two girl friends: Mary, who lives in town Z, and Nancy, who lives in town Y. Which is Tom likely to visit more often?

22. Which answer choice (a, b, or c) best completes the quotation?

"I do not know what I may appear to the world, but to myself I seem to have been only a boy playing on the sea-shore, and diverting myself in now and then finding a smoother pebble or prettier sea shell than ordinary,
_____ ,,
Brewster's *Memoirs of Newton*

- (a) Whilst the great wave of Einstein's theory prepared to engulf my petty discoveries.
- (b) Whilst the great ocean of truth lay all undiscovered before me.
- (c) Whilst the bigger boys discovered boulders of infinite truth.

23. Which drawing (a, b, c, or d) is the opposite of the first?

                  a   b   c   d

24. Which items go in which boxes? Can you think of appropriate terms to replace the question marks?

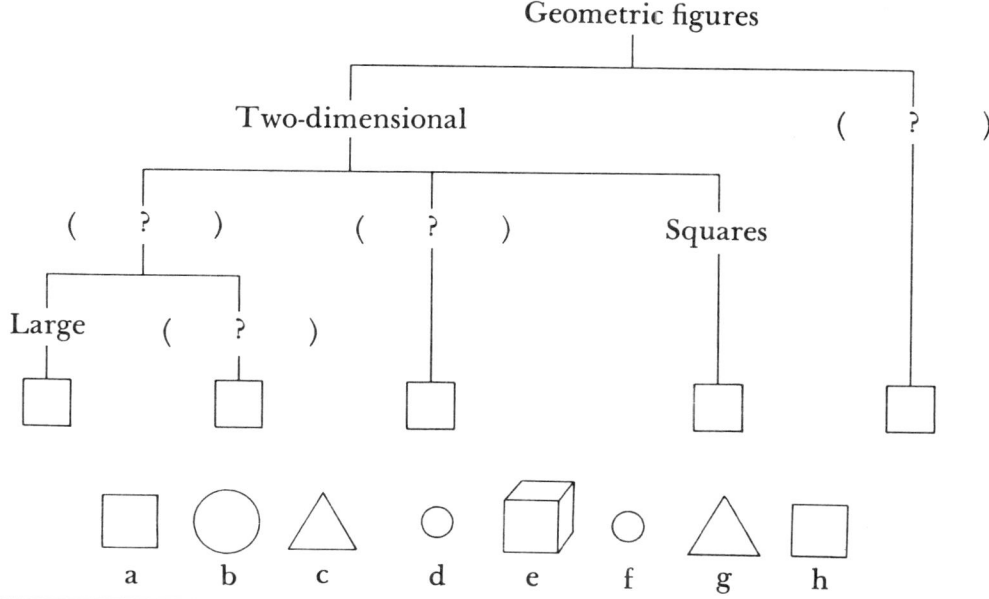

25. Choose the metaphorical term (a, b, c, or d) which you feel best completes the sentence. There is no "right" answer; pick the term which seems best to you.   Death is the _____ of life.

   (a) broken chain,   (b) overdrive gear,   (c) unborn seed of the withered flower,   (d) intermission

26. Which object (a, b, c, or d) is the same as the one at left?

   a   b   c   d

27. How many words does the square contain? (a) six, (b) seven, (c) eight, (d) no answer is possible until the word *word* is defined, (e) none; the words are in a rectangle, not a square

   MAT
   CAT TREE
   ANT WOMAN
   CAT TOP

28. Which object (a, b, c, or d) is the opposite of the one at left? Why?

   a   b   c   d

29. Which drawing (a, b, or c) belongs in the same class with the two at left?

   a   b   c

30. If the present sequence continues, what will the remainder of the graph look like?

   a   b   c   d

31. Match each use of the word *volume* with the corresponding meaning, at right.

The *volume* is nine cubic centimeters.	A	a		Book, especially one of a series.
Turn down the *volume*.	B	b	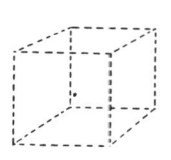	Quantity of space bounded by three dimensions.
"Once upon a midnight dreary, while I pondered, weak and weary, Over many a quaint and curious *volume* of forgotten lore..." Edgar Allan Poe, *The Raven*	C	c		Degree of loudness.
As the transaction *volume* mounts, accounting controls increase in importance.	D	d		Quantity, amount or number of something.

32. Which object (a, b, c, or d) is the same as the one at left?

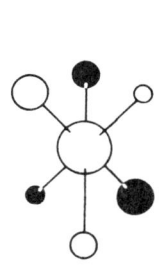

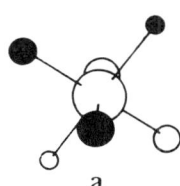
a

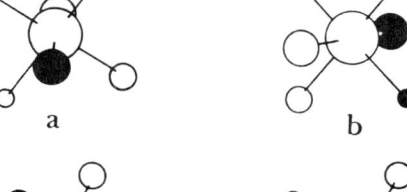
b

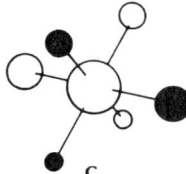
c

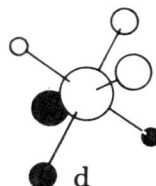
d

33. How many ways can you think of to get a raise in salary? Develop a classification, starting with the methods illustrated below. Think of at least five additional ways.

Ask nicely

Work hard

---

34. Choose the metaphorical term which you feel best completes the sentence. There is no "right" answer; pick the term which seems best to you.   Swearing is _____.
(a) rotten language, (b) spicy sauce in the bland stew of ordinary speech, (c) a verbal miscarriage, (d) the putrid excrement of a constipated mind

---

35. Match each use of the word *moon* with the proper meaning, at right.

"Hey diddle diddle,
The cat and the fiddle,
The cow jumped over the
   moon..."
     Mother Goose's Melody
	A a	 
		The natural satellite of any planet.

"What in its ruddy orbit lifts the blood,
Like a perturbed *moon* of Uranus,
Reaching to some great world in
  ungauged darkness hid."
     Coventry Patmore,
     The Unknown Eros
	B b	 Earth's natural satellite.

"You saw the moon from Sussex Downs, A Sussex moon, untravelled still, I saw a *moon* that was the town's, The largest lamp on Campden Hill." G. K. Chesterton, *The Napoleon of Notting Hill,* dedication	C c	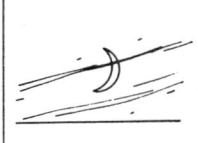 The appearance of Earth's satellite at a particular time.

36. Can you make up appropriate terms for the blank spaces of the outline?

> A. Preparing for computations
>   1. _____
>   2. Listing values of symbols
>   3. _____
> B. _____
>   1. Computations within parentheses
>   A. _____
>   1. Dividing 18 by 2
>   2. _____
>   B. _____
>   2. _____

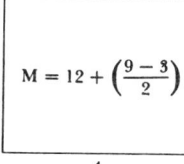
1

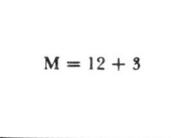
2

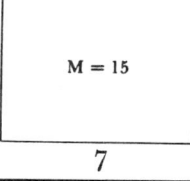
3

4

$M = 12 + \left(\frac{6}{2}\right)$
5

$M = 12 + 3$
6

$M = 15$
7

37. Choose the word (a, b, or c) which completes the analogy.

HUNGARY / ___ = ___ / POLAND   RUSSIA   COMMUNISM

                                      a   b   c

38. If the tip of South America is a horn, and Italy is a boot, what is New Guinea? Can you make up a descriptive name?

---

39. Which answer choice (a, b, c, or d) is the opposite of the two circles?

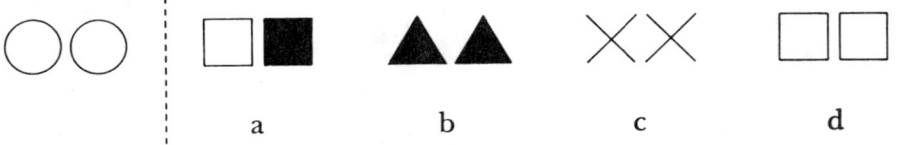

---

40. Which object (a, b, or c) goes in the same class with the two at left?

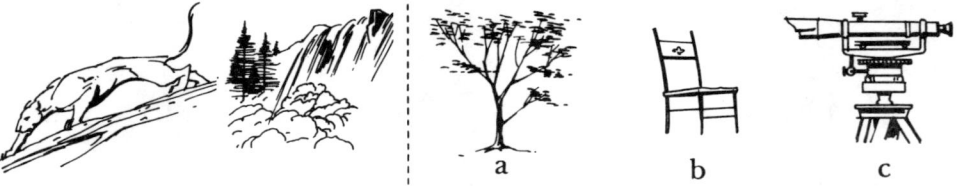

---

41. Write three sentences using the word *fall* in three different senses: first as a verb, second as a noun, third as an adjective.

---

42. Which drawing (a, b, c, or d) is the opposite of the one at left?

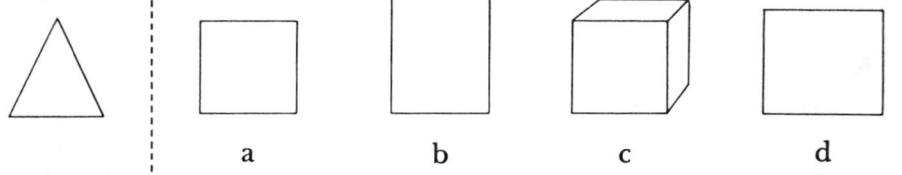

---

43. Which letter (a, b, c, or d) is the opposite of the one at left?

S	N	E	W	S
	a	b	c	d

44. What idea does this incomplete analogy give you? How might you plan a meal, thinking in this way?

$$\frac{\text{SONG}}{\begin{array}{l}\text{FIRST VERSE}\\ \text{CHORUS}\\ \text{SECOND VERSE}\\ \text{CHORUS}\\ \text{Etc.}\end{array}} = \frac{\text{DINNER}}{?}$$

45. Make a structure analysis diagram of the circle at right. Below is a sample structure analysis diagram of another figure.

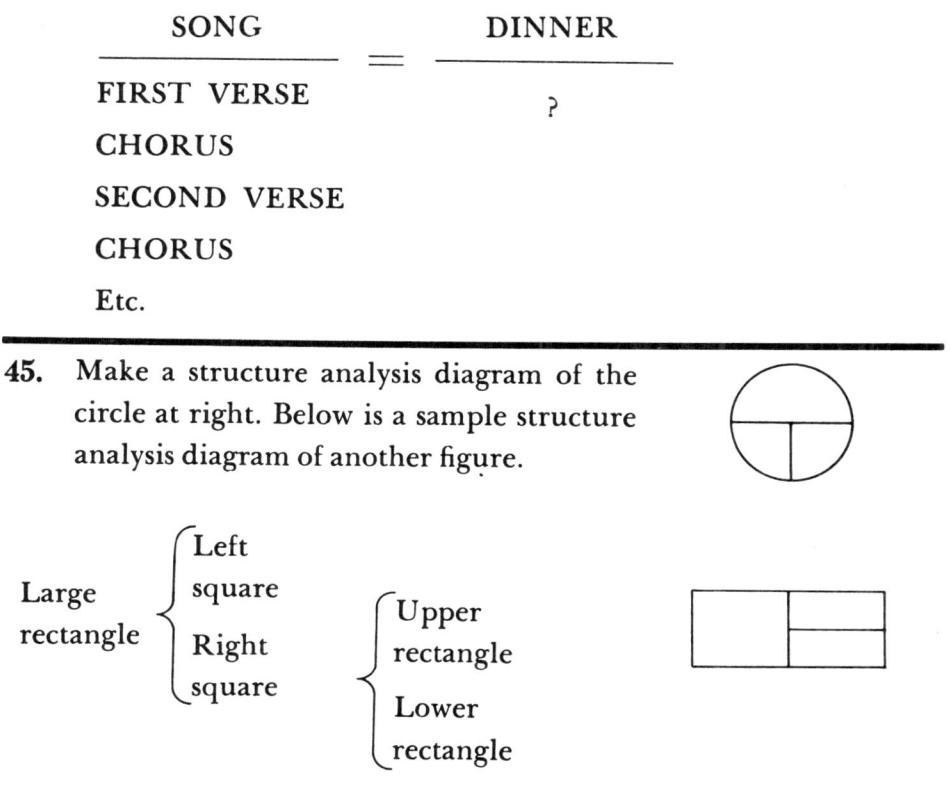

Large rectangle { Left square, Right square { Upper rectangle, Lower rectangle } }

46. Mrs. Jones went to the grocery store and bought some bacon, apples, potatoes, butter, bread, lamb chops, pears, corn, milk, rolls, oranges, and lettuce. The meat cost twice as much as the produce (fruits and vegetables). The baked goods cost one third less than the dairy products. The fruits cost 50 per cent more than the vegetables. The dairy products cost three times as much as the vegetables. The lamb chops cost $2.90 The corn cost ten cents less than the potatoes. The milk cost eleven times as much as the lettuce. The potatoes cost forty cents. The milk cost $1.80 less than the lamb chops. What was the total cost of the groceries? Hint: This problem can be simplified by the use of a classification diagram.

47. Make a classification diagram of the objects pictured below. For example, if you were classifying various types of food in a grocery store, you might make a diagram such as the one shown. Remember that any group of objects may be classified in different ways according to different purposes. Since this exercise has no purpose, you may classify the objects below however you wish.

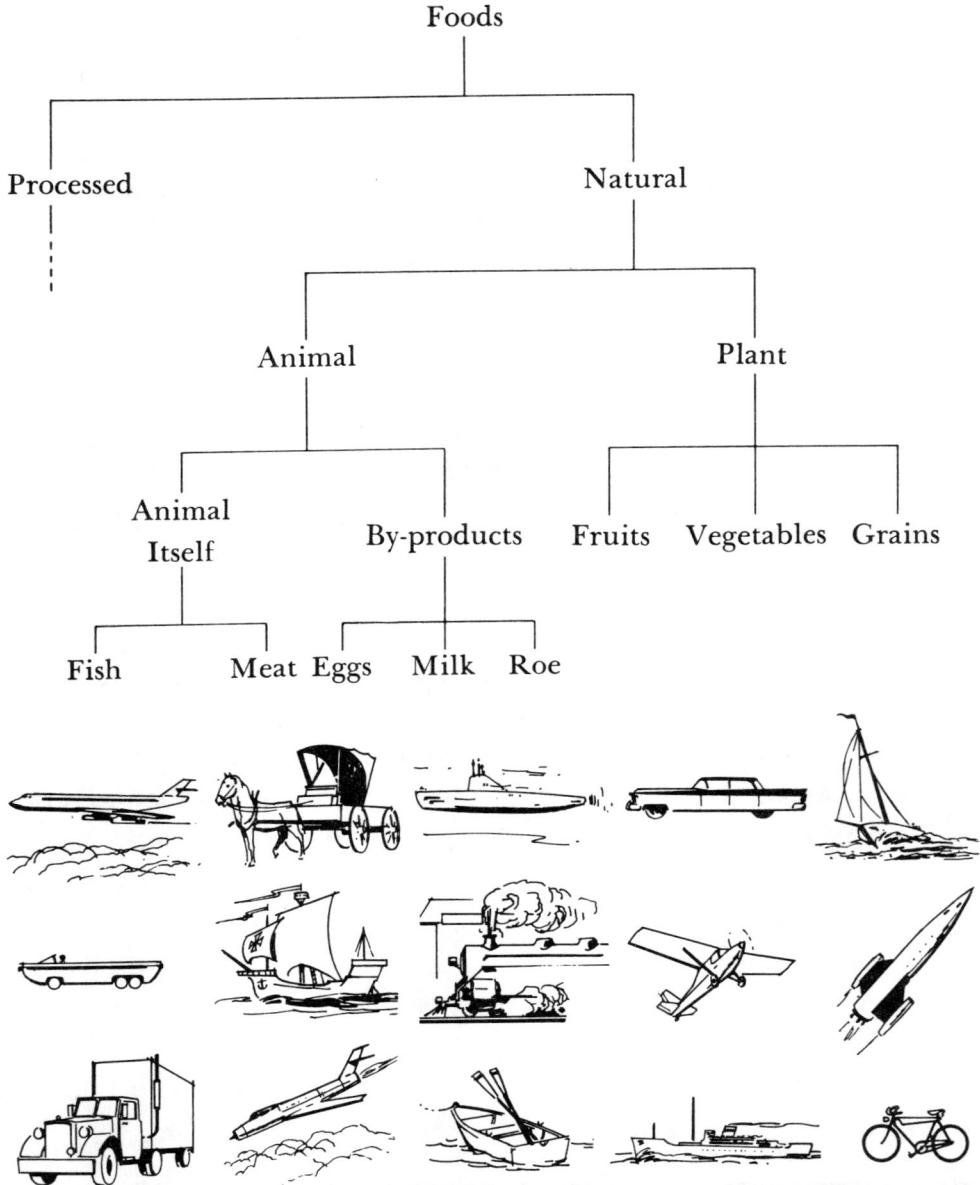

48. Write a sentence using the word *lamp* as the name of part of something. Then write another sentence using *lamp* as the name of the whole object.

49. Which item (a, b, or c) completes the analogy?

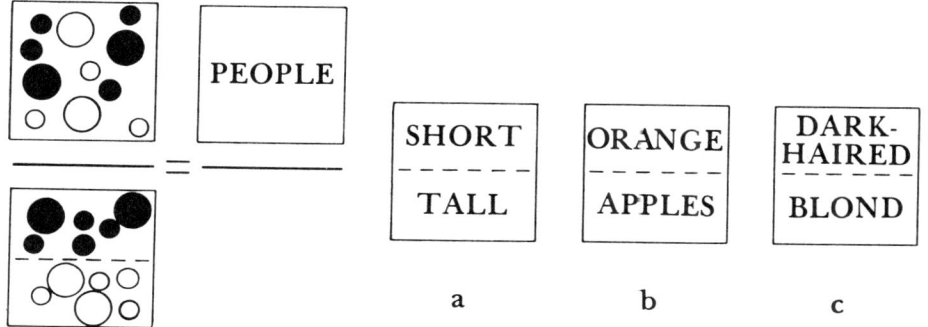

50. Which drawing (a, b, c, or d) is the same as the one at left?

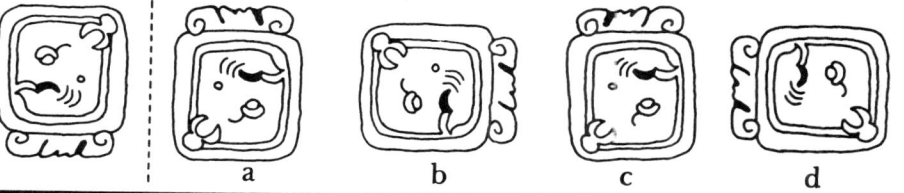

51. Make an operation analysis of the sequence below. For example, if you were to think of the stages of a man's life, you might make an operational outline, such as the one at right.

Man's life
1. Birth
2. Life
    1. Childhood
    2. Youth
    3. Adulthood
3. Death

a a a b b b C C C D D D

52. Match each use of the word *flower* with the proper meaning, at right.

She plucked the *flower* from its stem.	A a		Flowering plant.
"A simple maiden in her *flower* is worth a hundred coats-of-arms." Alfred, Lord Tennyson, *Lady Clara Vere de Vere*	B b		A figure of speech, as, "The Lord is my shepherd."
This *flower* has bifurcate leaves.	C c		Blossom.
"The poet knows that he speaks adequately, then, only when he speaks somewhat wildly, or 'with the *flower* of the mind.'" Ralph Waldo Emerson, *The Poet*	D d		Period of flourishing; youth.

53. Which answer choice (a, b, or c) completes the analogy? Why?

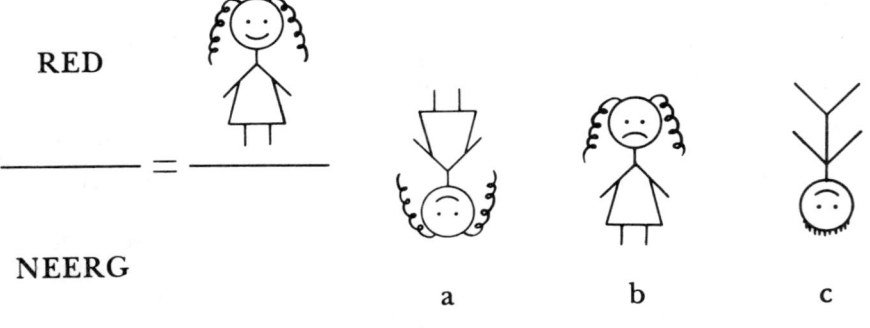

54. How does the meaning of *helix* shift, from the first sentence to the second?   A *helix* is a spiral, such as the path of a screw's thread. A snail is a type of *helix*, a spiral-shelled mollusk.

(a) by qualification (thing to quality),   (b) by structure analysis (part to whole),   (c) by qualification (quality to thing)

55. Which drawing (a, b, or c) belongs with the two at left?

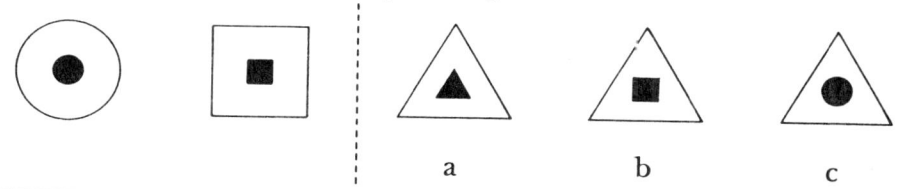

a   b   c

56. This exercise illustrates that classification can facilitate the creation of new procedures. Continuing the classification diagram below, list two or more additional methods of drawing a circle. Think of an entirely new method, if you can.

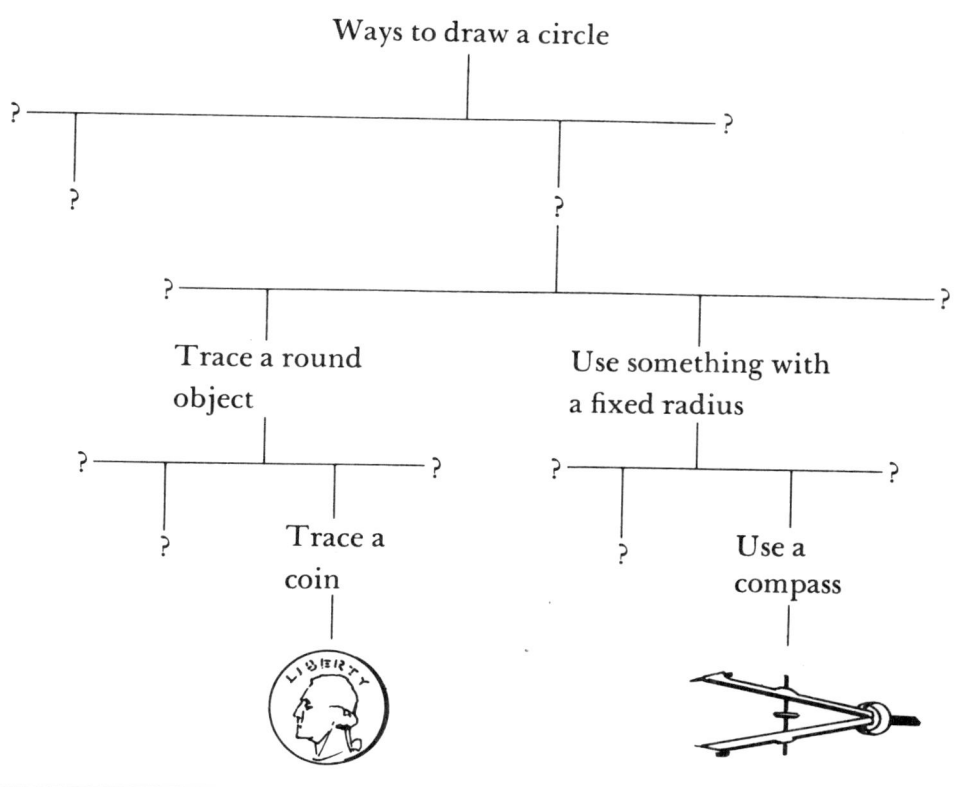

LEVEL 5
Medium−Difficult

1. Which answer choice (a, b, c, or d) belongs in the blank space of the series?

        XX1X5XX2XXX4X3XXX3X_____X2XXXX5XX1XXX

X5X	4XX	XXX	XX6
a	b	c	d

2. Which item (a, b, or c) goes in the blank space of the analogy?

3. Think of three or more meanings of the word *property*.

4. Which is the largest object?
Which is the smallest?

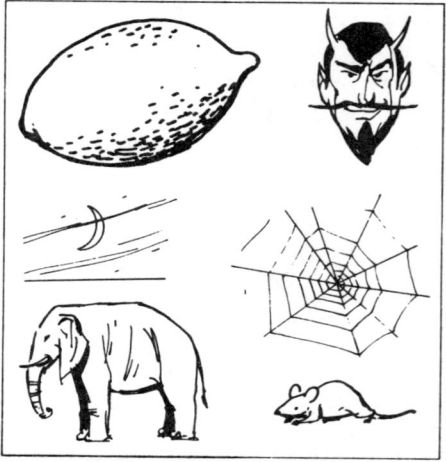

5. Which drawing (a, b, c, or d) comes next in the sequence?

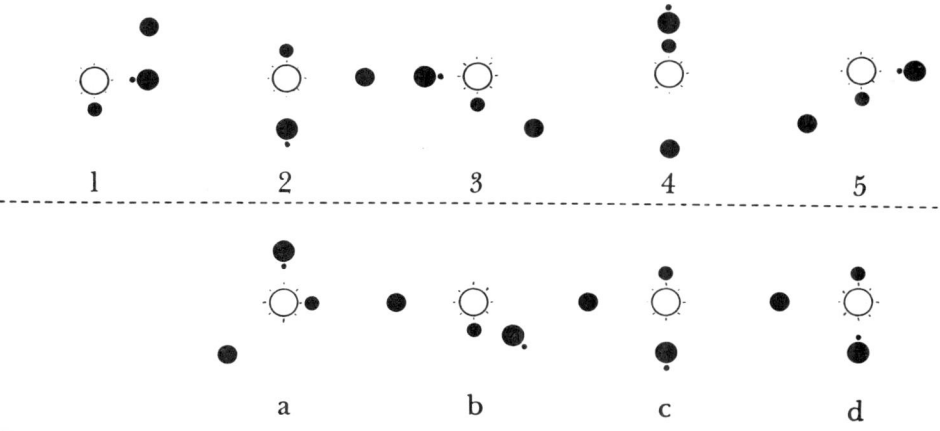

6. Think of several senses of the word *bar*.

7. What type of quality does each box show? Sensory, emotional, or logical?

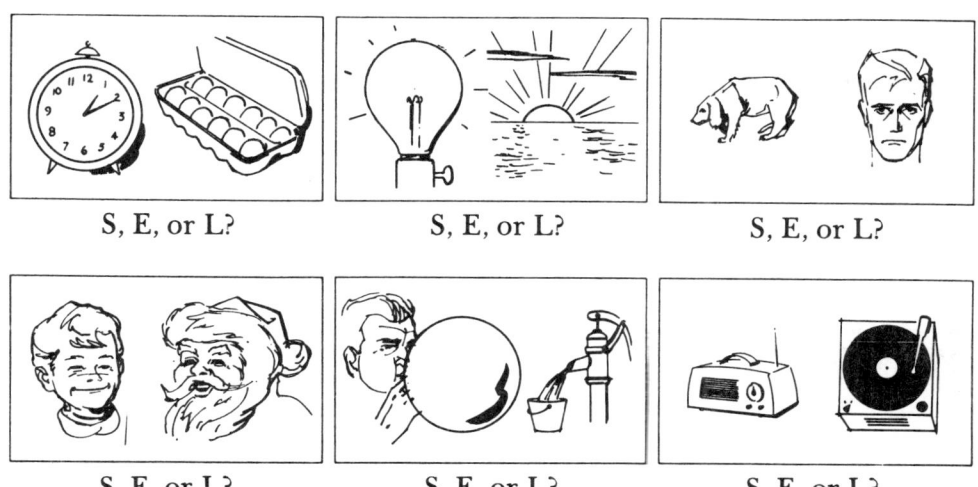

8. Which object (a, b, or c) goes in the same class with the two at left?

　　　a　　　　b　　　　c

9. Which word (a, b, c, or d) is the opposite of the first?

RED	YELLOW	BLUE	COLOR	VIOLET
	a	b	c	d

10. Which pair of words (a, b, c, or d) is the opposite of the pair at left?

WHITE BLACK	HOT COLD	BAD EVIL	CAUTIOUS BOLD	FAST SLOW
	a	b	c	d

11. Which drawing (a, b, or c) belongs with the two at left?

　　　a　　　　b　　　　c

12. Which word (a, b, or c) completes the analogy?

$$\frac{\text{COIN}}{\text{DIME}} = \frac{\quad\quad}{\text{DOLLAR}} \quad\quad \text{QUARTER} \quad\quad \text{MONEY} \quad\quad \text{BILL}$$

　　　　　　　　　　　　　　a　　　　　b　　　　c

13. Think of five or more meanings of the word *sun*. Consider that this word may be the name of a specific thing, a general class of things, a quality, an action, a metaphorical thing, etc.

14. What word should replace the question mark?

"Humility, that low, sweet root
From which all heavenly virtues shoot."
              Thomas Moore, *The Loves of the Angels*

Stems, leaves, etc. of a plant		All heavenly virtues
shoot from	(both) originate from	have as their motivating source
Low root		(?)

15. Which object (a, b, c, or d) is the opposite of the first?

16. Match each use of the word *man* with the proper meaning, at right.

"The Simiadae then branched off into two great stems, the New World and the Old World monkeys; and from the latter at a remote period, *Man*, the wonder and the glory of the universe, proceeded." Charles Darwin, *The Descent of Man*	A a	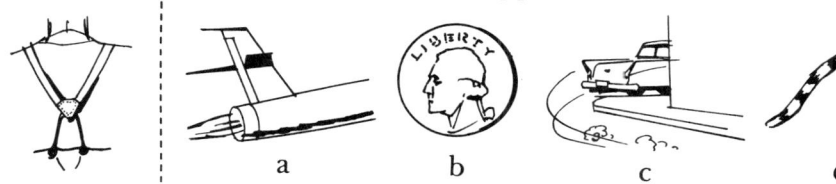 Adult male human being.
"The Book of Life begins with a *man* and a woman in a garden." Oscar Wilde, *A Woman of No Importance*	B b	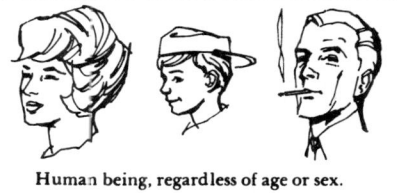 Human being, regardless of age or sex.
"To every *man* upon this earth death cometh soon or late." Thomas Macaulay, *Lays of Ancient Rome. Horatius*	C c	 Human beings collectively, mankind.

17. All things (whether people, automobiles, or mollusks) can be classified according to sorting factors — named qualities. Can you name the qualities by which things are sorted into classes, or types? In the diagram below, what is the sorting factor at X? At Y? What quality is ignored?

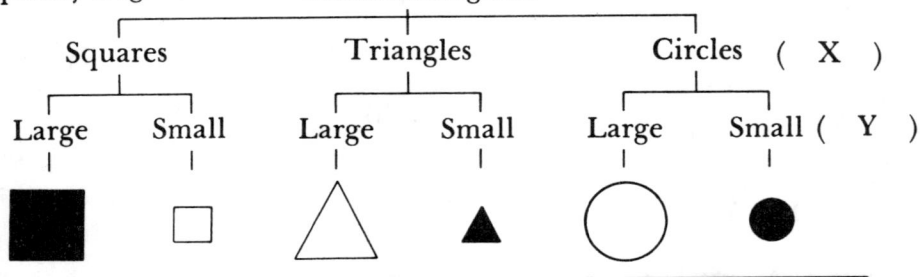

18. A concept may be thought of in terms of many different metaphors. For example:

>Memory is an attic.
>Memory is a fishing net.
>Memory is a refrigerator.

How else might we think of memory? Think of several additional ways.

>Memory is ____?____ .

19. How many "things" can you "make" of the random dots at right? Can you see lines, squares, triangles, trees, faces? Now look at the scene before you: your room or the view from your window. How many ways can you perceive this same scene?

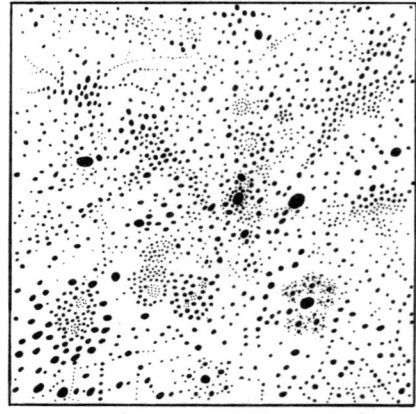

20. Match each use of the word *space* with the proper meaning, at right.

But will it fit in the *space* available?	A a	A length of time; an interval between two points of time.
A Russian, not an American, was the first man to enter *space*.	B b	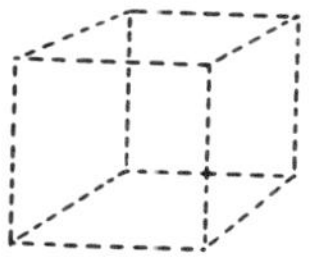 A distance, area or volume between things or limits.
The *space* between birth and death is much too short.	C c	 Outer space, the universe beyond Earth's atmosphere.
"Somewhere, beyond *space* and time, Is wetter water, slimier slime..." Rupert Brooke, *Heaven*	D d	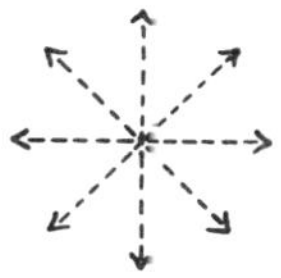 The unbounded volume of nothingness in which objects reside; opposite of matter.

21. Which item (a, b, or c) completes the analogy?

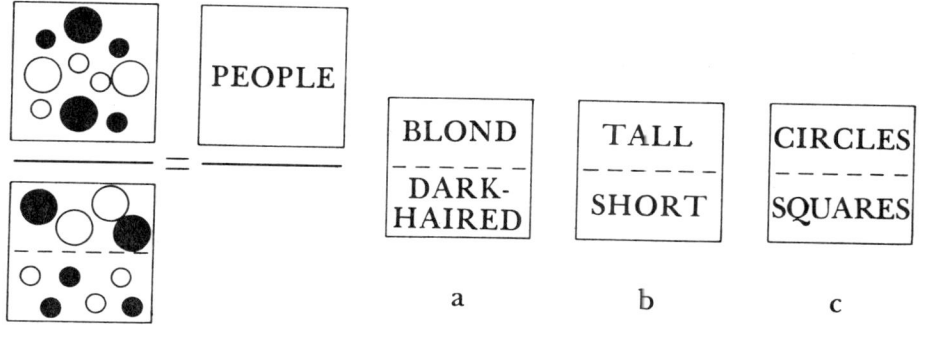

22. Which object (a, b, or c) belongs with the two at left?

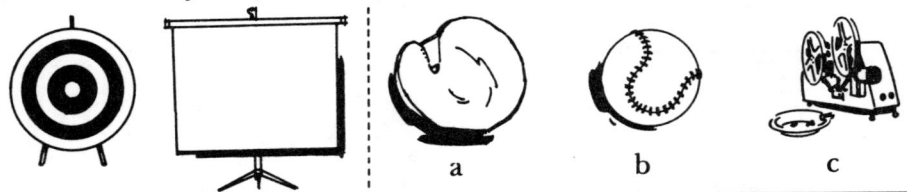

23. Make up a new meaning for the word *nozzle*.

24. Into what stages and sub-stages might you divide this operation?

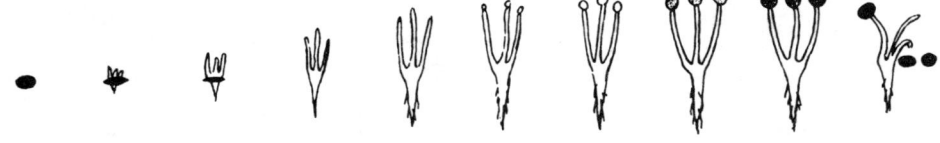

25. Is *state* a synonym of *nation*?

    (a) yes   (b) no   (c) sometimes

26. Study the figure below for three or four minutes. Then sketch it from memory on a separate sheet of paper.

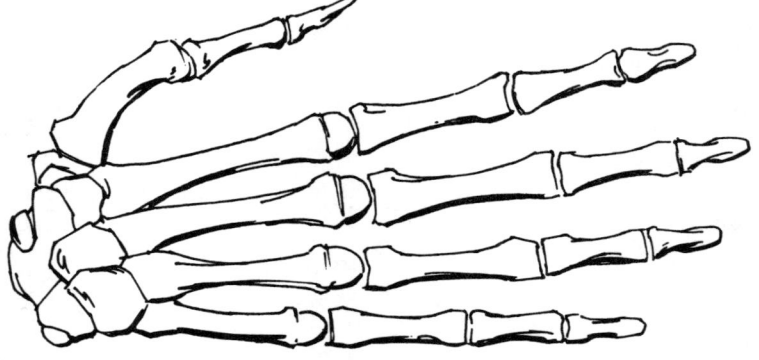

27. Which words go in which spaces of the structure analysis diagram? Take the words from the map. One of the words has already been correctly placed.

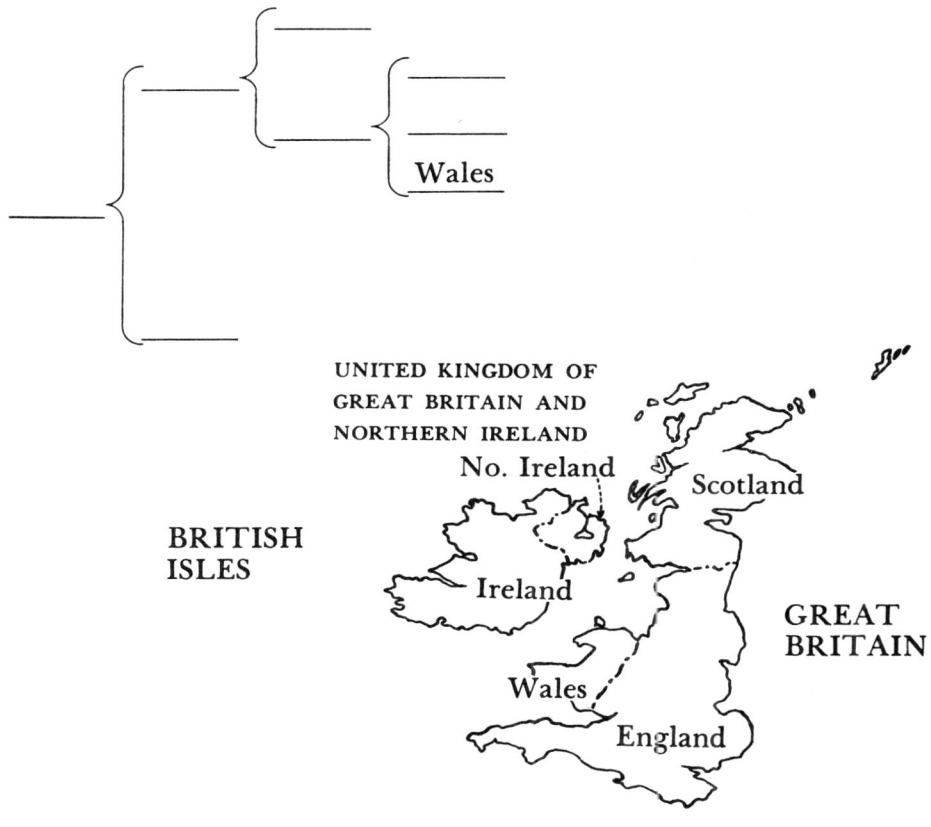

28. Albert kissed Jan seven times. Jan kissed Albert five times. How many times did they kiss each other? If the answer is five, which of the following is the most probable meaning of *kiss*?

   (a) Caress with the lips (by one person).
   (b) Reciprocal caress with the lips between two people.
   (c) A gesture with the lips, not involving physical contact with another person, as "to throw a kiss."
   (d) A trace or small amount of something, as, "a kiss of lemon."

29. Make a classification diagram of types of weapons. A few weapons are shown below. Make your diagram complete enough to encompass these and at least ten other types. For example, if you were to classify footwear, you might make a diagram such as the one below.

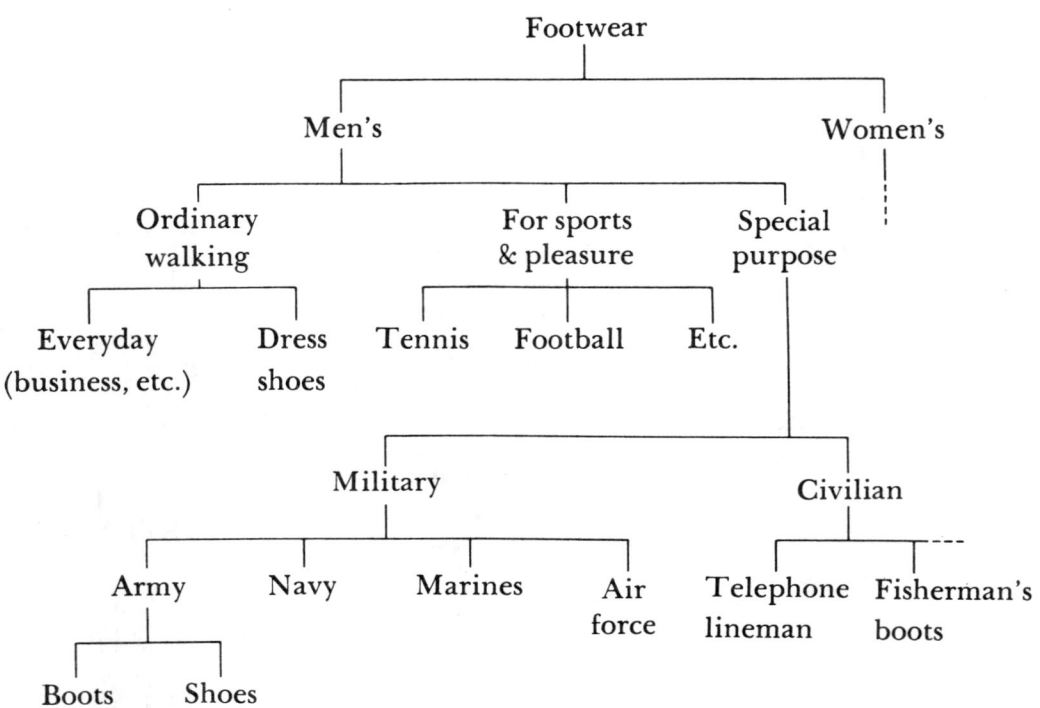

30. What idea does this incomplete analogy give you?

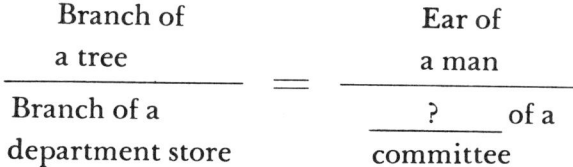

31. Which object (a, b, or c) belongs in the same class with the two at left?

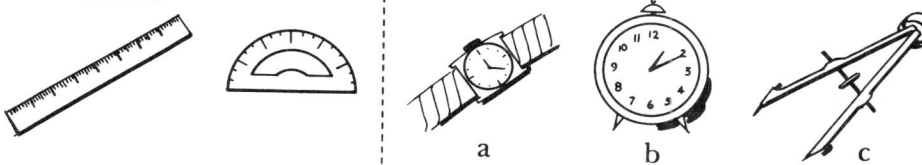

32. Which item (a, b, c, or d) is the same as the one at left?

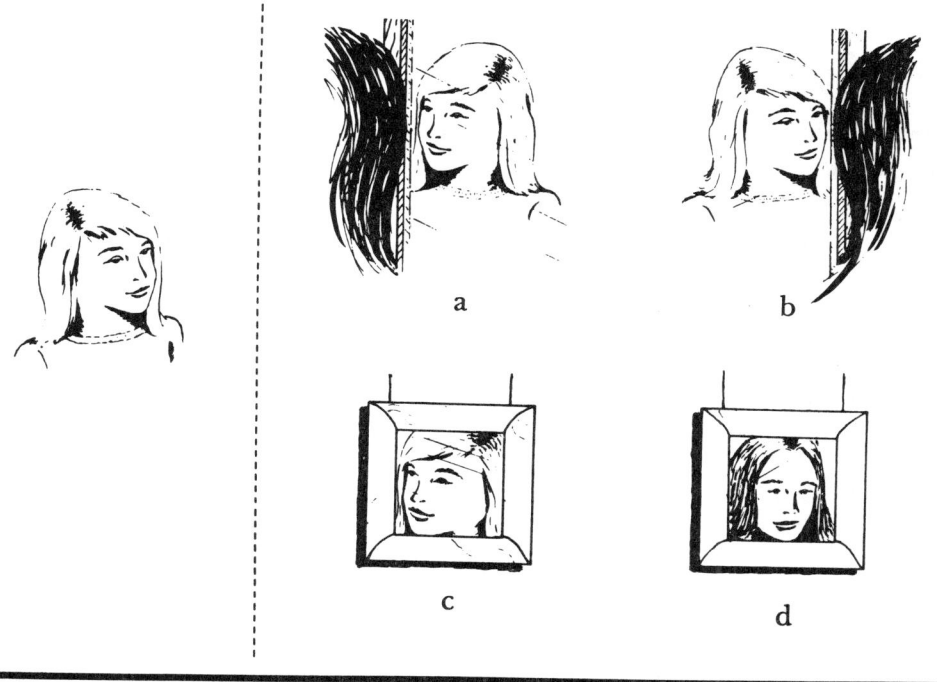

33. Match each use of the word *plant* with the proper meaning, at right.

Both sides of the river were dense with *plants* and trees.	A	a		A member of the vegetable kingdom.
He could not *plant* a blow squarely.	B	b		To place or land, as a blow.
"Persecution is a bad and indirect way to *plant* religion." Sir Thomas Browne, *Religio Medici*	C	c		The buildings, land, apparatus, etc., of an industrial firm.
Some plankton are animals, others are *plants*.	D	d		A soft-stemmed member of the vegetable kingdom, as opposed to a shrub or tree.
The *plant* is worth much more than the inventory.	E	e		To establish, found, settle, inculcate, as a colony or an idea.

34. Which quotations (on this and the next page) belong in which boxes?

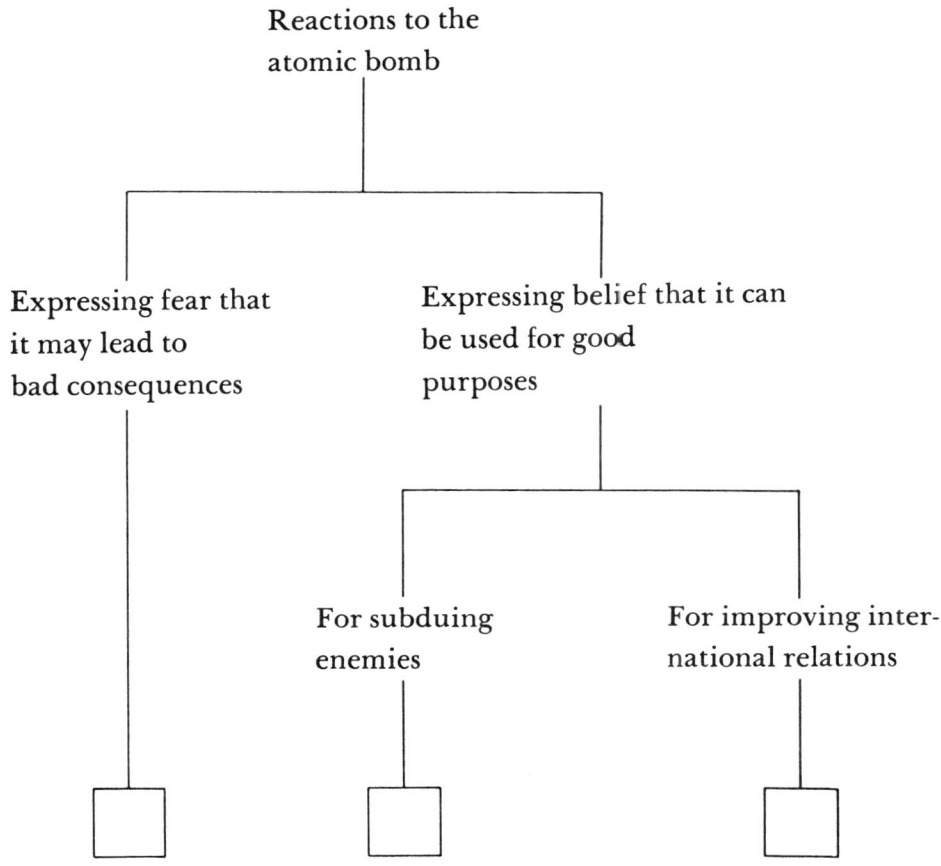

A. "Since I do not foresee that atomic energy is to be a great boon for a long time, I have to say that for the present it is a menace."
    Albert Einstein, "Einstein on the Atomic Bomb,"
    Atlantic Monthly (November, 1945)

B. "The bomb that fell on Hiroshima fell on America too. It fell on no city, no munition plants, no docks. It erased no church, vaporized no public buildings, reduced no man to his atomic elements. But it fell, it fell. It burst. It shook the land. God, have mercy on our children. God have mercy on America."
    Hermann Hagedorn, *The Bomb That Fell on America*

C. "We turned the switch, we saw the flashes, we watched them for about ten minutes — and then we switched everything off and went home. That night I knew that the world was headed for sorrow."

                Leo Szilard, Speech at 80th anniversary of *The Nation*

D. "Sixteen hours ago an American airplane dropped one bomb on Hiroshima. . . . It is a harnessing of the basic power of the universe. The force from which the sun draws its powers has been loosed against those who brought war to the Far East."

                Harry S. Truman, First announcement of the dropping of the
                atomic bomb, August 6, 1945

E. "Nothing could have been more obvious to the people of the early twentieth century than the rapidity with which war was becoming impossible. And as certainly they did not see it. They did not see it until the atomic bombs burst in their fumbling hands."

                H. G. Wells, *The World Set Free*

F. "It [the atomic bomb] may intimidate the human race into bringing order into its international affairs, which, without the pressure of fear, it would not do."

                Albert Einstein, "Einstein on the Atomic Bomb,"
                Atlantic Monthly (November, 1945)

35. Does this incomplete analogy give you an idea? What other analogies might you construct, to help you generate new thoughts?

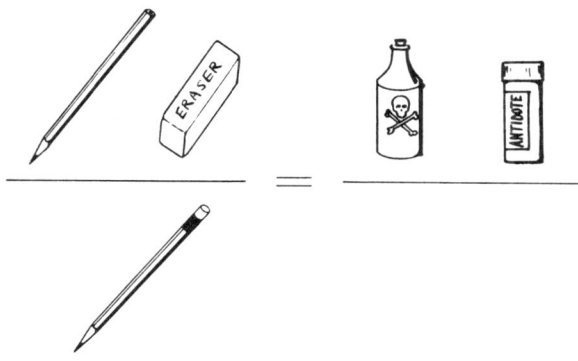

36. How does the meaning of *balance* shift, from the first sentence to the second?

>Scales are in *balance* when the opposing weights are equal.
>An account is in *balance* when the debits equal the credits.

(a) by classification (genus to species), (b) by analogy, (c) by thing-making (thing to similar thing)

37. Writing a novel, planning an invasion, running a factory: these and thousands of other happenings must be divided into stages (or "time parts") in order to be understood. This exercise gives practice in operation analysis. Make an outline of the happening illustrated below. A sample outline of pole vaulting is at right.

Pole vaulting
1. Running start
2. Vault
   A. Lift self to bar
   B. Clear bar
   C. Release pole
3. Fall to sawdust

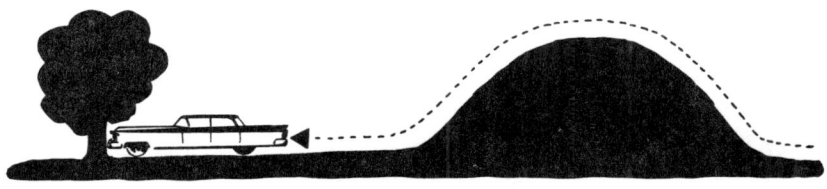

38. Which drawing (a, b, c, or d) comes next in the series?

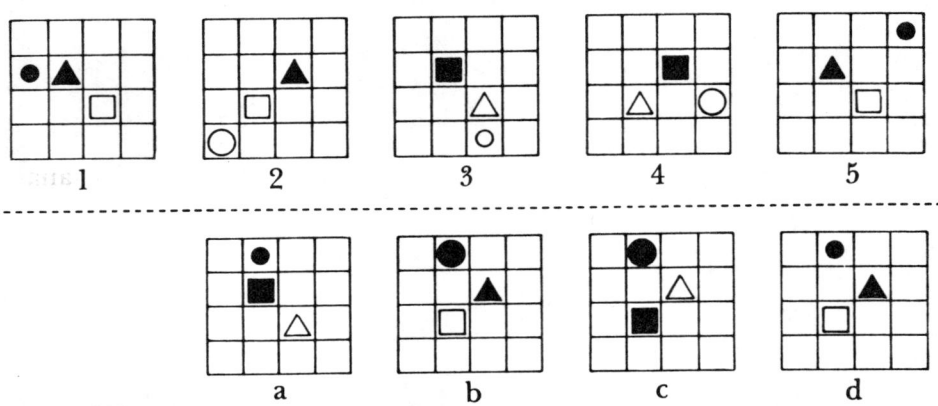

39. Which drawing (a, b, c, or d) is the same as the first?

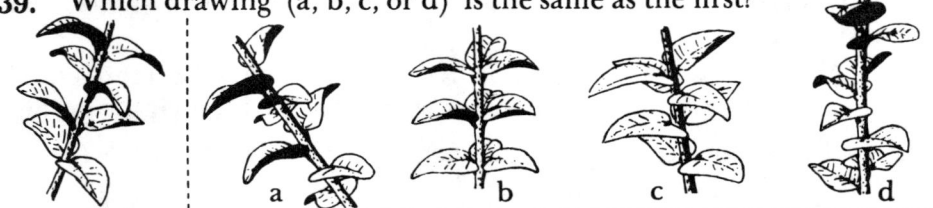

40. Study the word list for five or ten minutes. Then, on a separate sheet of paper, write as many of the words as you can remember. Hint: You can remember the words more easily if you classify them.

RED	MAN	CHILD	YELLOW
TWO	SIX	BOOK	PARALLEL
TRAILER	SWEET	ORANGE	WATER
LEMON	AVOCADO	LAWYER	SEED
NINE	OCEAN	SHRILL	COLOR
GREEN	FISH	BIRD	BEAR
LIZARD	TOMATO	APPLE	ORANGE
SEAL	BULL	TREE	SALMON
MOTHER	PEAR	PLANT	WOMAN
FAWN	BLUE	WHEEL	SEVEN

41. Classification can be an aid to "creativity" — sparking new ideas, inventions, methods. By making use of the classification diagram below, can you think of a new "location" for a timepiece? A clock may be placed on a shelf or set in a wall; a watch may be worn on the wrist. What other locations are possible? Can you think of an entirely new location? The classification diagram suggests how you might guide your developing thoughts.

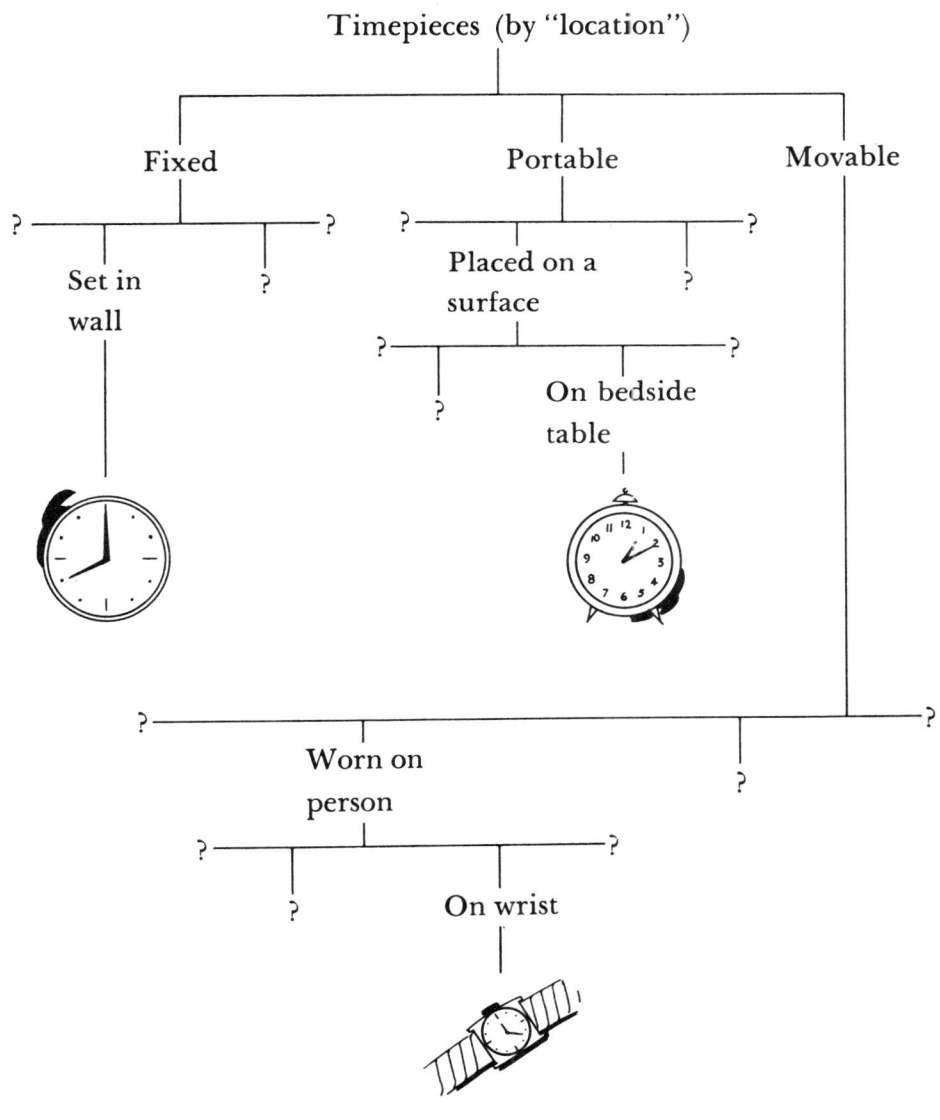

LEVEL 6
Difficult

1. Which answer choice (a, b, c, or d) comes next in the series? Try dividing the sequence into stages, as if it were an operation.

    XOXOXOXXOXOOXOXOXXXOXOXOXXXOXOXO
    XXOXOOXOXOXXXOXOXOXOXXXOXOXOXXOXOO
    XOXOXXXOXOXOXXXOXOX_____

XOOXO	XOXOX	XXOXX	OXXOX
a	b	c	d

2. Pick the object (a, b, c, or d) which is the opposite of the first.

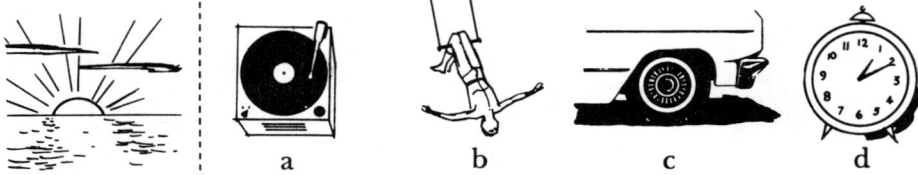

a   b   c   d

3. Make a structure analysis diagram of the figure at right. For example, if you were to analyze the structure of a man, you might make a diagram such as the one below. Though this exercise may be of little value in itself, it is intended to give you practice in how to analyze *any* structure.

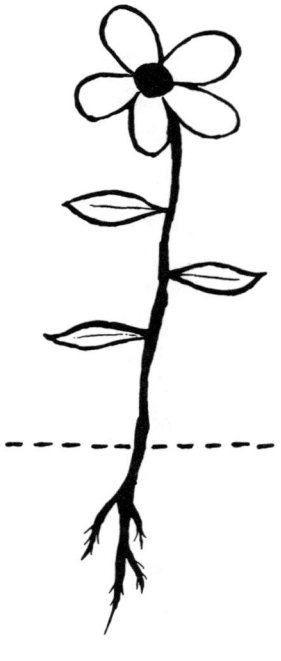

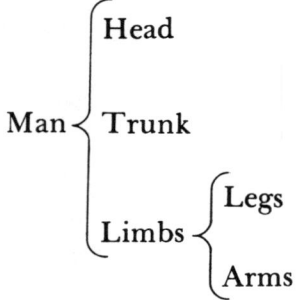

4. Think of five or more senses of the word *shell*.

5. Which drawing (a, b, or c) completes the analogy?

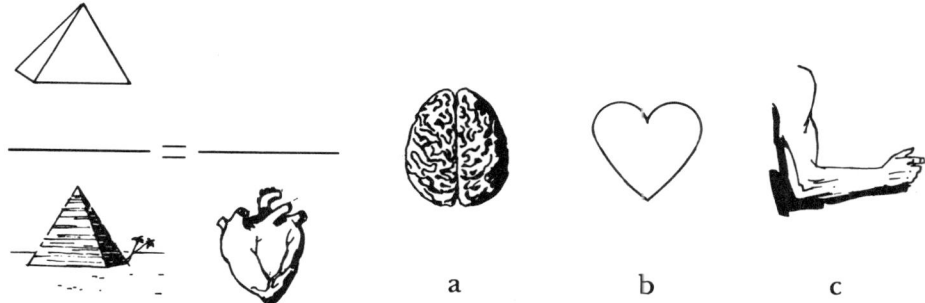

6. How does the meaning *of stroke* shift, from the first sentence to the second?   He took a short *stroke*, then turned for the last lap. His best *stroke* is the Australian Crawl.

(a) by operation analysis, (operation to part), (b) by operation analysis (stage to operation),   (c) by classification (species to genus)

7. Through the centuries, men have mentally linked the stars into patterns: the Big Dipper, the Southern Cross, the Great Bear. Imagine that the dots at right are stars. What "constellations" might you create?

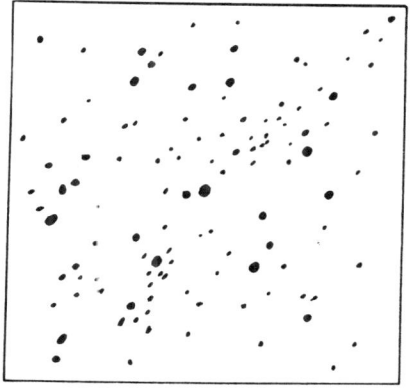

8. How many squares are at right?

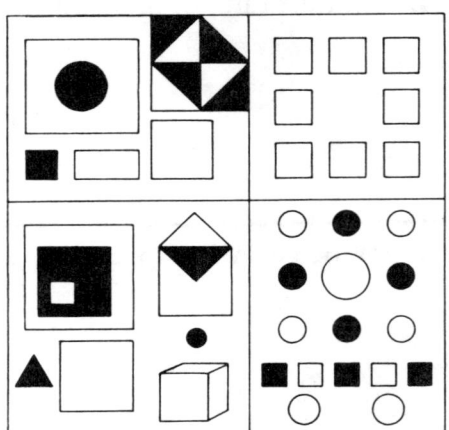

9. Which drawing (a, b, or c) belongs with the two at left?

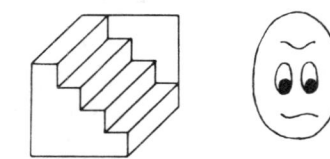  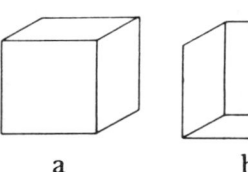

                                                           a   b   c

10. Can you replace the two question marks with appropriate words?

"Worry, the interest paid by those who borrow trouble"
    George Washington Lyon, Epigram in *Judge* (March 1, 1924).

Interest		(?)
is paid by those who borrow	(both) must be endured by those who obtain	is suffered by those who anticipate
(?)		Trouble

11. Which object (a, b, c, or d) is the same as the first?

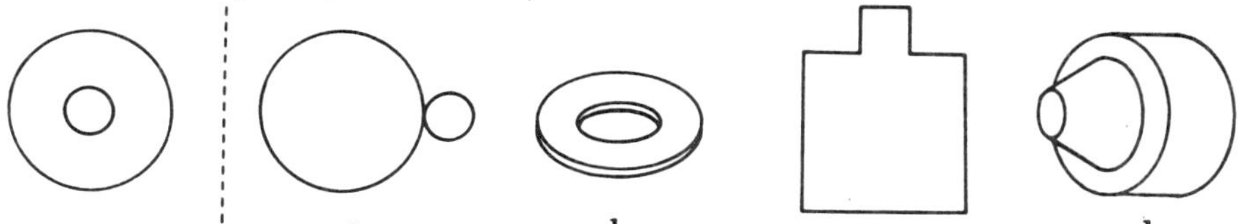

12. The last word of this sentence is _____.

13. Which answer (a, b, or c) goes with the two objects at left?

14. Which set of words (a, b, c, or d) is the opposite of the set at left?

TOE	TWIG	PLANET	WORD	EARTH
FOOT	BRANCH	SOLAR SYSTEM	SENTENCE	UNITED STATES
LEG	TREE	GALAXY	PARAGRAPH	TEXAS
	a	b	c	d

15. Which word (a, b, or c) completes the analogy?

$$\frac{\text{HOUR}}{\text{DAY}} = \frac{\text{HORSES}}{\quad}$$ MARES   ANIMALS   CARNIVORES

                                            a   b   c

16. Can you invent a new type of mirror? List several qualities of the mirror shown. These qualities may suggest other possible qualities.

17. How many men are there in a town composed of the following: 3,500 adults; 4,750 children; 4,050 males; 4,200 females? If the answer is 8,250, what is the definition of the word *man*?

    (a) A human being
    (b) The human race
    (c) A male human being
    (d) An adult male human being
    (e) A male servant

18. How does the meaning of *mother* shift, from the first sentence to the second?   John's *mother* is fifty-three years old.
    Where is the colt's *mother*?

    (a) by operation analysis (stage to operation),   (b) by structure analysis (whole to part),   (c) by classification (species to genus)

19. Which item (a, b, or c) completes the analogy?

20. Make a classification diagram of the quotations below. How might such a diagram help you to grasp and to judge the various points of view?

A. "Human life consists in mutual service. No grief, pain, misfortune, or 'broken heart' is excuse for cutting off one's life while any power of service remains. But when all usefulness is over, when one is assured of an unavoidable and imminent death, it is the simplest of human rights to choose a quick and easy death in place of a slow and horrible one."

     Charlotte Perkins Stenson Gilman, *Note written before her suicide*

B. "a suicide is a person who has considered his own case and decided that he is worthless and who acts as his own judge jury and executioner and he probably knows better than anyone else whether there is justice in the verdict"

 Donald Robert Perry Marquis, *archy does his part. now look at it*

C. "Razors pain you;
Rivers are damp;
Acids stain you;
And drugs cause cramp.
Guns aren't lawful;
Nooses give;
Gas smells awful;
You might as well live."

  Dorothy Parker, *Résumé*

D. "O! that this too too solid flesh would melt,
Thaw and resolve itself into a dew;
Or that the Everlasting had not fix'd
His canon 'gainst self-slaughter!"

  William Shakespeare, *Hamlet*

E. "Man is a prisoner who has no right to open the door of his prison and run away.... A man should wait, and not take his own life until God summons him."

  Socrates, *Dialogues of Plato. Phaedo*

21. How many types of headdresses can you name? Develop a classification, starting with the items shown below. Think of at least five additional types of coverings for the head. Though you may not have a keen interest in hats, crowns, and the like, remember that this exercise is intended to sharpen your ability to generate and organize ideas of *any* type.

22. Which object (a, b, or c) belongs with the two at left?

                                    a   b   c

23. Can you replace the three question marks with appropriate words? The word or phrase in the middle box should indicate what the relations in the other two boxes have in common.

"Boldness is a mask for fear, however great."
Lucan, *Book IV, The Civil War.*

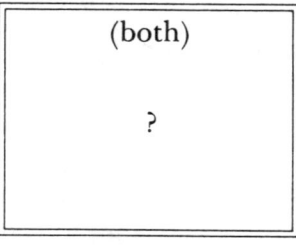

24. "Words often grow new senses. For example, the word *squeak* comes from the word *mouse*." Is this an accurate statement?

25. Which answer choice (a, b, or c) continues the series?

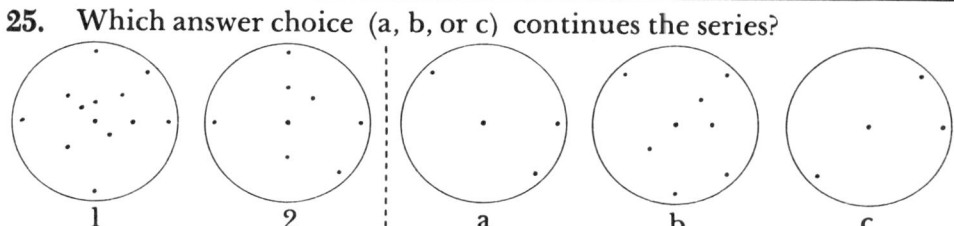

1   2   a   b   c

26. If you were God, what types of creatures might you create, other than those which now exist? Three possibilities are shown below. "Create" at least five others.

27. Which drawing (a, b, c, or d) is the same as the one at left?

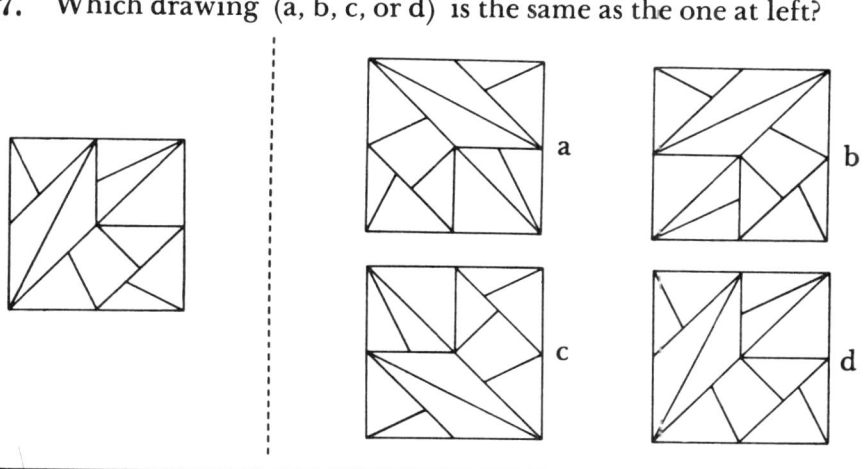

28. The United States is made of states and the states are made of counties. Similarly, operations are made of stages and the stages are made of sub-stages. How good are you at identifying the constituent "parts" of happenings? Make an outline of the operation pictured below. Your outline should indicate stages and sub-stages. For example, if you were to analyze the "operation" of a year, you might make an outline such as the one at right.

 Year
  Spring
   March
    March 21
    March 22
    Etc.
   April
   May
   June
  Summer
  Autumn
  Winter

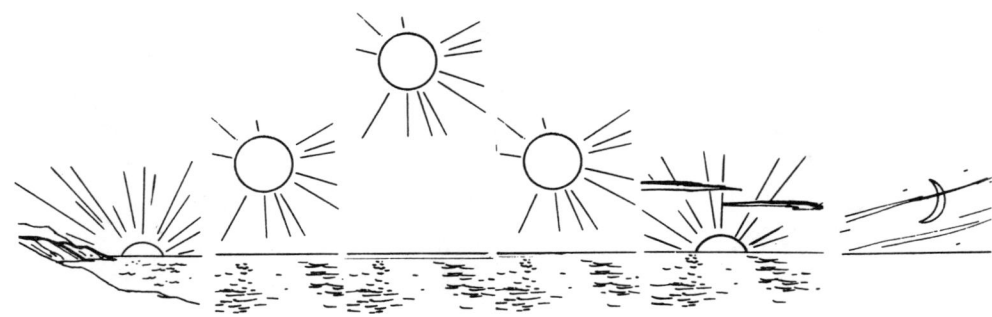

29. Which pair (a, b, c, or d) is the opposite of the one at left?

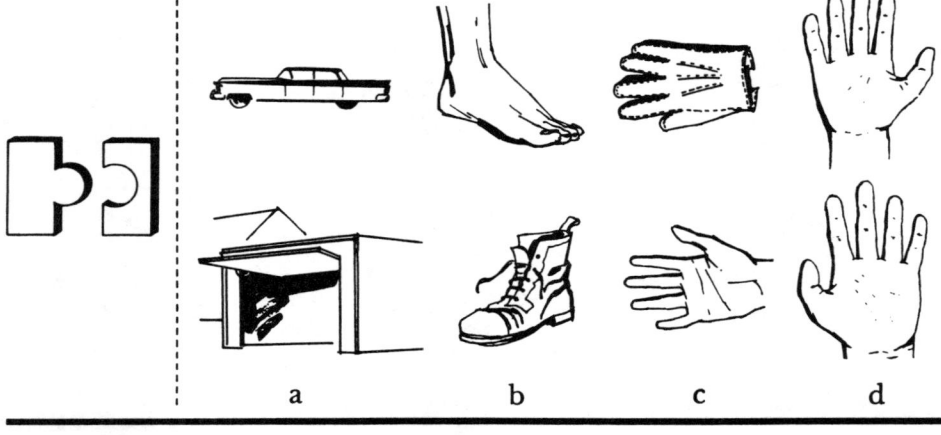

     a   b   c   d

30. Study the drawing for five or ten minutes. Then sketch it from memory on a separate piece of paper. Hint: In studying the drawing, you might find it helpful to make use of a structure analysis diagram; at least you must *think* structurally — of parts within parts.

31. Can you think of two meanings of the word *year,* one of which includes the other? Hint: You may have to leave Earth.

32. Which answer (a, b, or c) belongs in the same class with the first two groups?

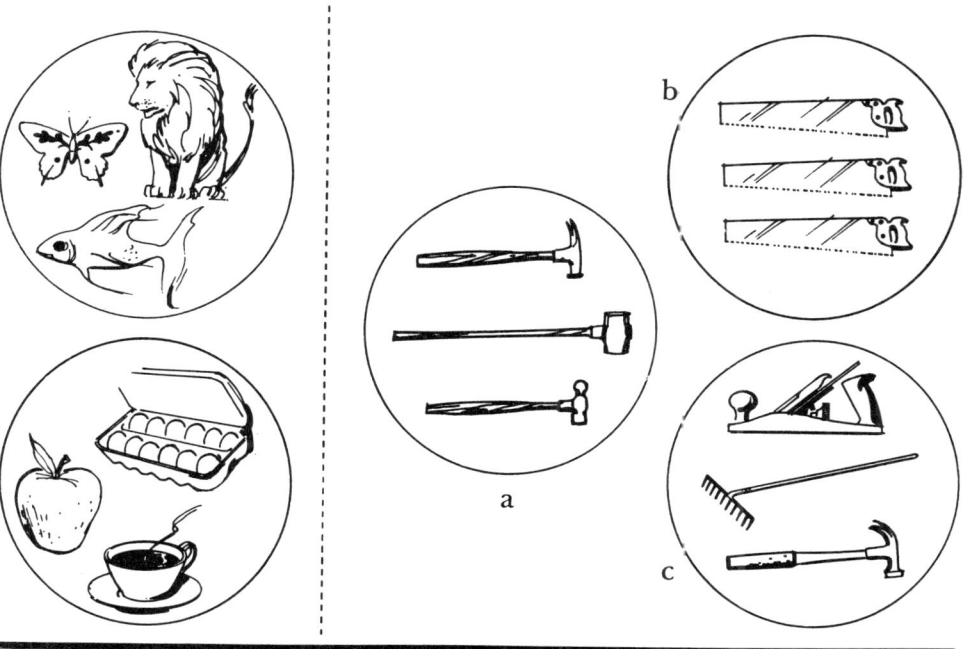

33. Match each use of the word *train* with the appropriate meaning, at right.

A. "*Train* up a child in the way he should go: and when he is old, he will not depart from it." Proverbs	a	A trailing stream.
B. They *trained* their guns on the condemned man, firing in unison.	b	A number of people following an example, as if they were the retinue of a prince.
C. "The Son of God goes forth to war, A Kingly crown to gain; His blood-red banner streams afar: — Who follows in his *train*?" Bishop Reginald Heber, *The Son of God Goes Forth*	c	A connected sequence, succession, or series.
D. She interrupted his *train* of thought.	d	Railroad cars, pulled by one or more locomotives.
E. "Glorious the sun in mid-career; Glorious th' assembled fires appear; Glorious the comet's *train* . . ." Christopher Smart, *Song to David*	e	To educate, instruct, rear.
F. "*Train* up a fig-tree in the way it should go, and when you are old sit under the shade of it." Charles Dickens, *Dombey and Son*	f	To aim or direct.
G. "Sure, the next *train* has gone ten minutes ago." *Punch*, vol. lx, (1871)	g	To direct growth by pruning, bending, binding, etc.

34. The idea that books contain knowledge may be expressed in many ways. For example:

> Books are reservoirs of knowledge.
> Books are guardians of knowledge.
> Books are messengers of knowledge.

Think of several additional ways to express the relation between books and knowledge.

> Books are _____?_____ of knowledge.

35. A microphone magnifies faint sounds so that they may be heard. If you were President of the United States, what sort of "microphone" might you use to detect the first signs of trouble in foreign lands? If you were President, what other analogies might you use to solve your problems?

36. Things become meaningful to us only when we observe similar and different qualities among them. Often the different qualities far outweigh the similar ones. The realization of this fact may have prompted Lewis Carroll (in *Alice in Wonderland*) to ask, "Why is a raven like a writing desk?" If you cannot answer this question, try these easier ones. Why is "a" like "b"; "c" like "d"; "e" like "f"?

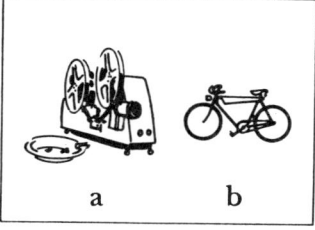
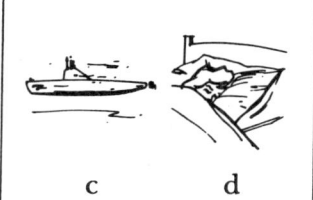
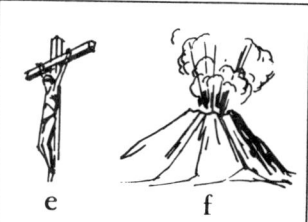

37. Does this partial analogy give you an idea about how crime might be prevented?

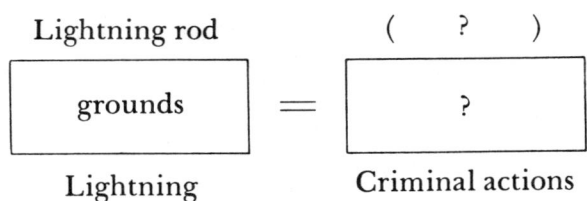

38. Which answer choice completes the series?

43254A3654bC765dEf87GhIj____

8KlMnO	6kLmNo	65KlMn	6KlMnO
a	b	c	d

39. In what ways can you express metaphorically the idea that most of Britain's former colonies have become politically independent? Examples:

    Most of Britain's children have left home.
    Most of Britain's colonial planets have ceased to orbit the British sun.
    Most of Britain's litter have ceased to nurse at the royal bosom.

Think of several other ways to express this idea.

    Most of Britain's _____?_____

40. An invention is often the result of filling out a classification in the mind. Can you "invent" a new source of illumination, by continuing the classification started below?

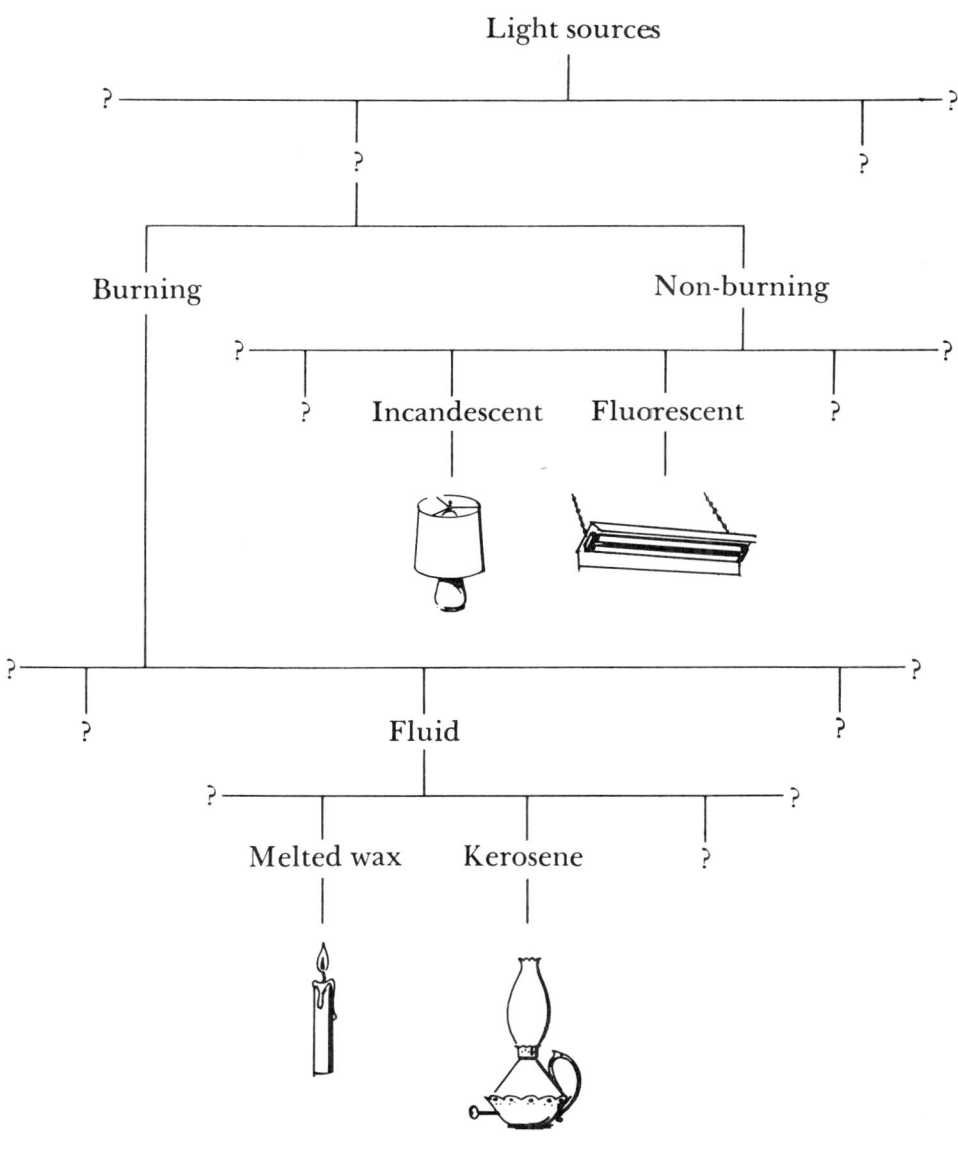

LEVEL 7
Very Difficult

1. Which item (a, b, c, or d) is the opposite of the first?

a b c d

2. Think of eight or more meanings of the word *part.*

3. Which term (a, b, c, or d) is the opposite of the one at left? Why?

	a	b	c	d
ABRAHAM LINCOLN	PENCIL	EIFFEL TOWER	TORONTO	NORTH POLE

4. How does the meaning of *church* shift, from the first sentence to the second?

"This *church* was built in 1923."
"She is active in the *church.*"

(a) by classification (genus to species), (b) by qualification (thing to quality), (c) by structure analysis (part to whole)

5. Which object (a, b, or c) belongs in the same class with the two at left?

a b c

6. Think of four or more meanings of the word *thing.*

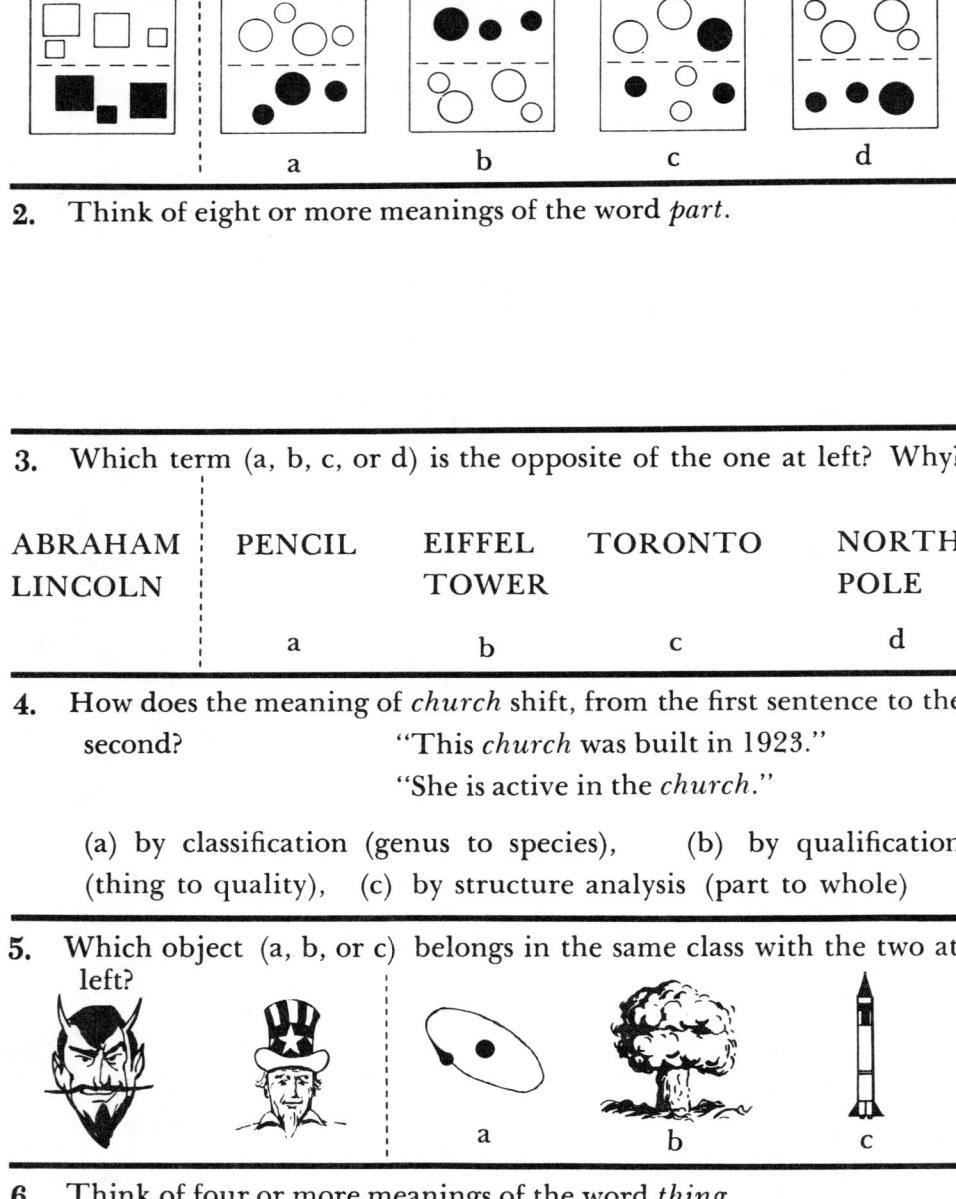

7. Study the sequence below for three or four minutes. Then reproduce it from memory on a separate sheet of paper.

1 2 1 2 A B A B 1 2 3 1 2 3 A B C A B C 9 8 7 6 5 6 7 8 9 Z Y X W V W X Y Z 1 B 3 D 5 F 7 H 9 J 2 L 4 N 6 P 8

8. Which drawing (a, b, or c) goes with the two at left? Why?

9. Which answer (a, b, or c) completes the analogy?

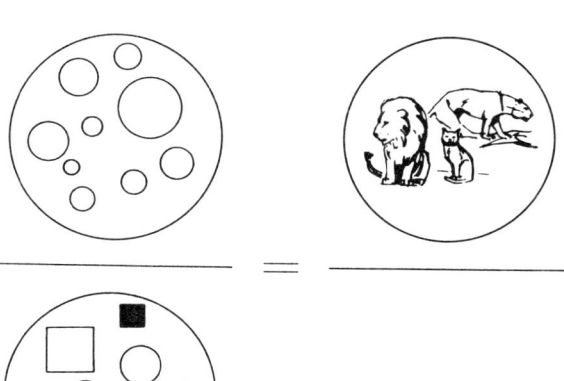

a

b

c

10. Make a classification of sorts of creativity, starting with the types shown below. Think of several additional types. What sorting factors might you use? Sensory mode? Type of "material"? Degree of intellect required? Usefulness to other people?

11. If a man's life is a strand, what is a rope? Why is a rope braided? What other analogies can you devise for thinking about a man's life?

12. Which item (a, b, c, or d) is the same as the one at left?

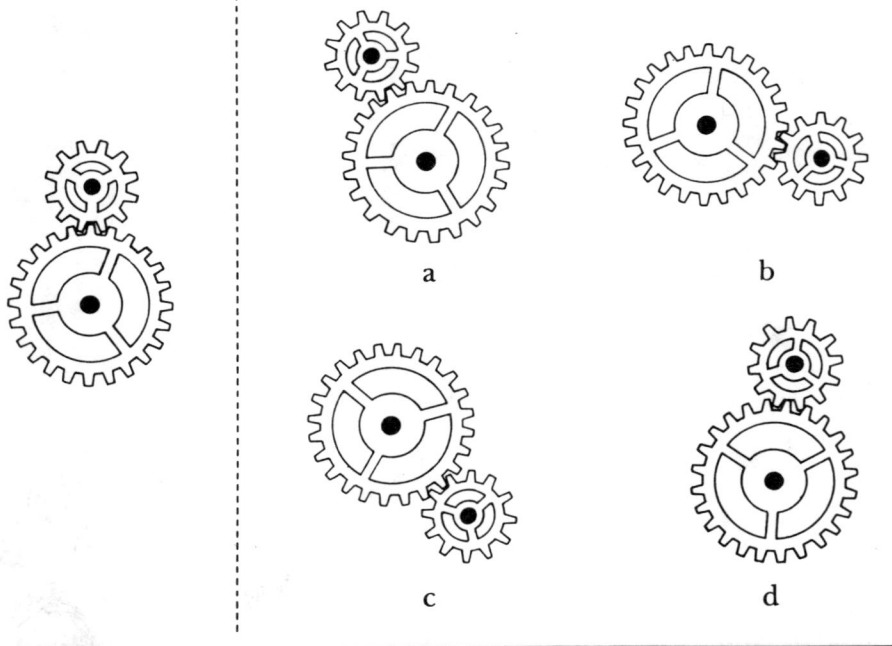

13. Make a structure analysis diagram of the map below. For example, if you were to analyze the structure of the solar system, you might make a diagram such as the one shown.

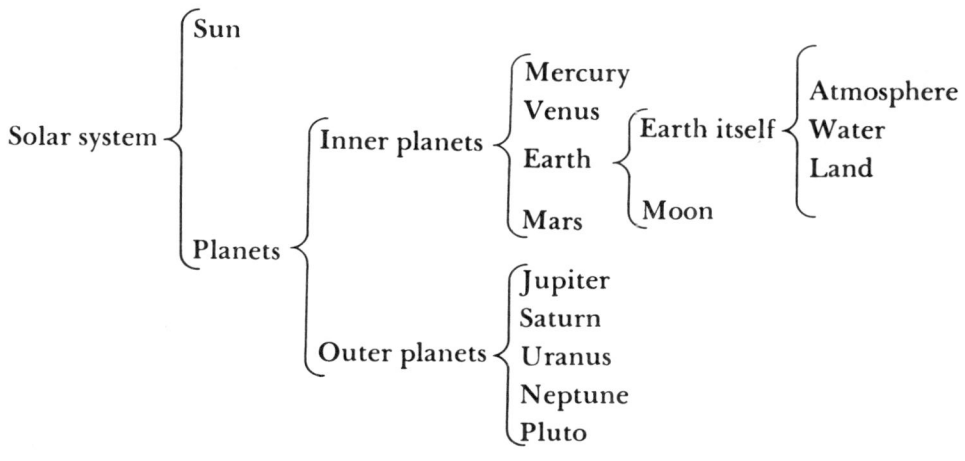

14. Which item (a, b, c, or d) is the opposite of the one at left?

Animal	Day	Quality	Paragraph	Tree
Mammal	Month	Color	Sentence	Branch
Dog	Year	Green	Word	Twig
	a	b	c	d

15. One of the words in the box is the most ambiguous in the English language. Which?

THING	LOVE
GOD	SET
POINT	FREEDOM
IN	SPACE

16. Define freedom.

17. Ice skates, roller skates, and skis are three types of footwear which enable one to "glide" over a surface. Can you invent another type? You might find it helpful to make a classification diagram. By this means, the similarities and differences of the existing items can suggest possible new items.

18. Which item (a, b, or c) belongs in the same class with the two at left?

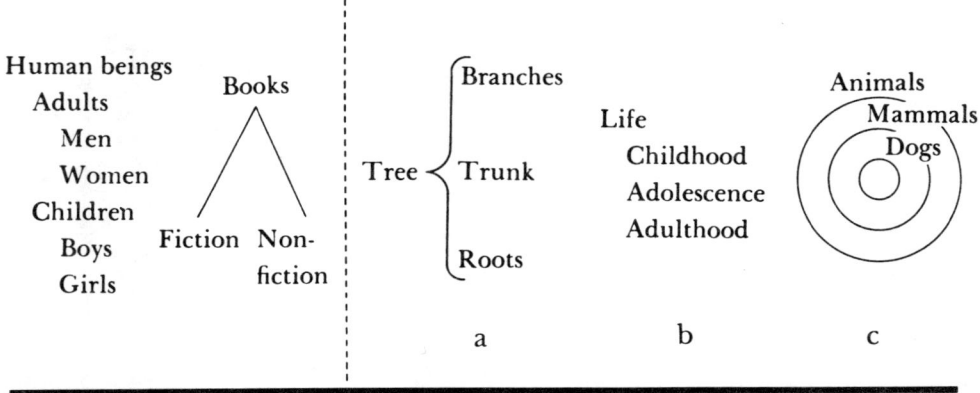

19. How many dots are in the box below? Can you count them accurately? This task (though meaningless in itself) is a good exercise in method. What *approach* can you devise?

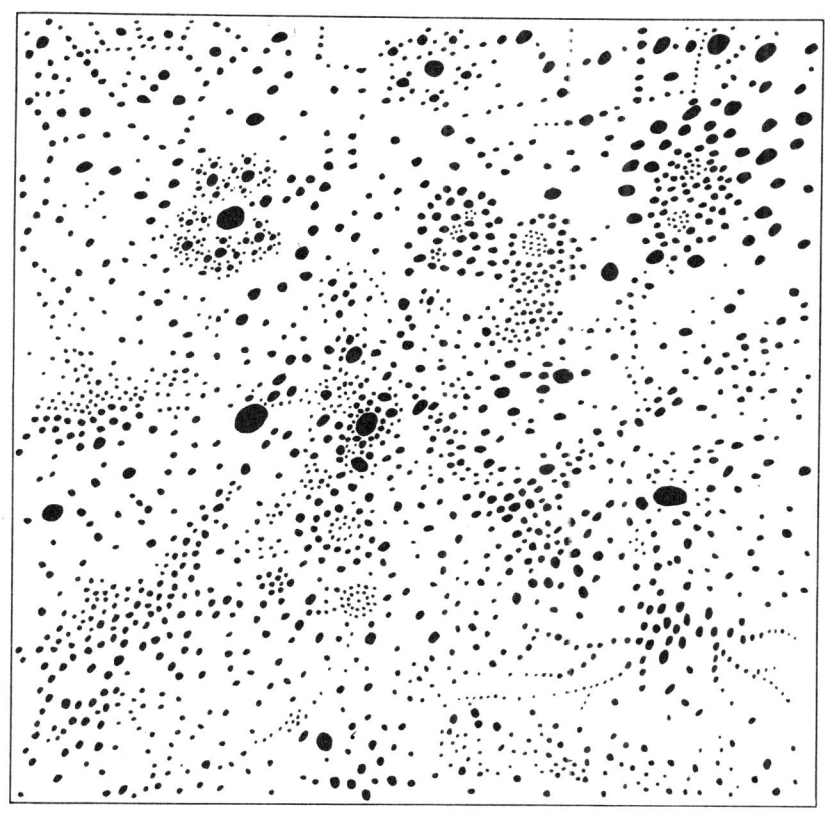

20. Which object (a, b, or c) completes the analogy?

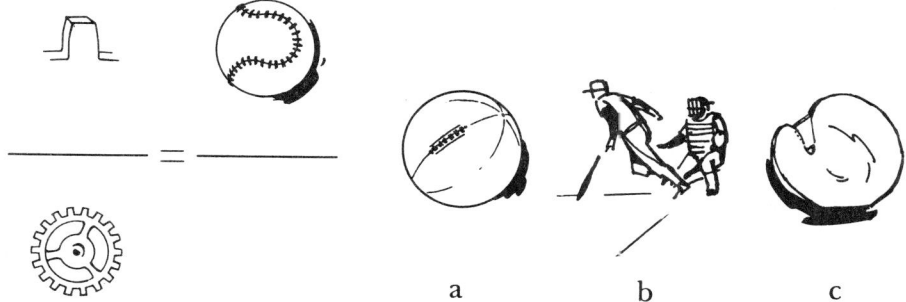

21. Make a classification diagram of the objects pictured below. Use whatever sorting factors you wish. For example: SIZE, LARGE, AIR, HABITAT, FOUR-LEGGED.

22. Which answer choice continues the sequence?

L03,501-33C; L05,504-99999; L12,509-2389HM98904B; L02, 521-21; L06,523-54987K; L19,529-47H3912457773225789; ____

L07, 536-046375N   L07,548-923847E
        a   c

L08, 548-5848372   L20, 520-HALT
        b   d

23. Under what conditions might a day have ten hours rather than twenty-four?

24. Can you replace the question marks with appropriate words? In the center box you should write a general phrase which includes the phrases in the other two boxes.

"A new deal for the American people."
            Franklin Delano Roosevelt

(?)   U.S. government

?   ?   provides new
                                laws and
                                policies for

(?)   (?)

25. Can you devise a new way to send a message, or to express something to someone? Perhaps so, perhaps not; but one way to go about it would be to develop a comprehensive classification of existing ways, and to look for "holes" in the classification — untried ways. You may use the partial classification below as a starting point.

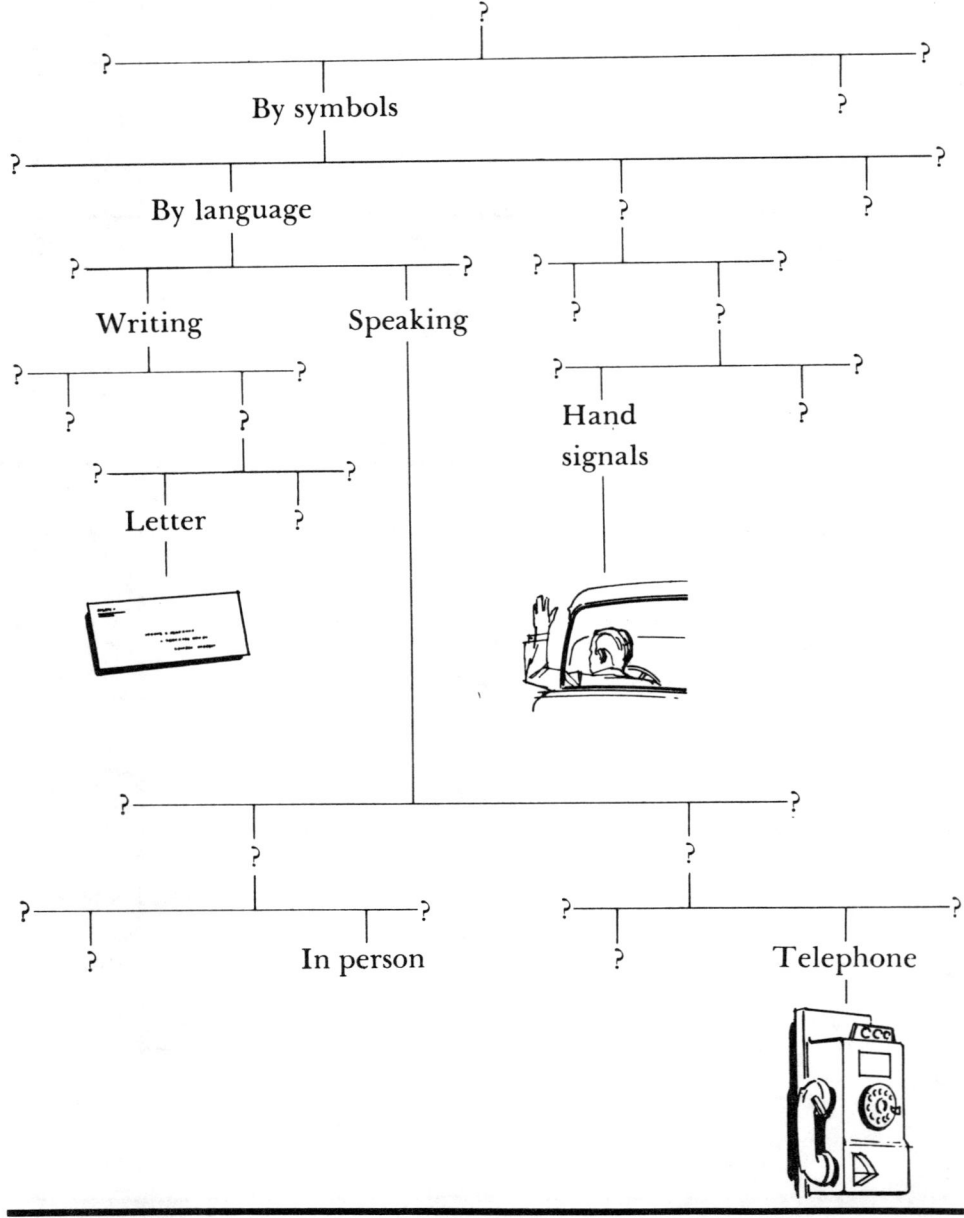

26. Many metaphors are used to describe God. We speak of Him as a *father*, as a *king,* and as a *lord*. Here are two other famous metaphors:

> The Lord is my *shepherd* ...
> A mighty *fortress* is our God, a *bulwark*
> never failing ...

Write an original metaphor describing God. Your metaphorical terms might be the names of men of various occupations; names of structures, such as buildings or bridges; or names of other things, qualities, or events.

27. Can you invent an improved type of ladder? You might find it helpful to make use of a structure analysis diagram. What parts and sub-parts do existing ladders have? What other parts and sub-parts are possible?

28. Can you replace the question marks with appropriate words? The middle box should contain a general relation which includes the relations in the other two boxes.

"The world state is inherent in the United Nations as an oak tree is in an acorn."

Walter Lippmann, One World or None

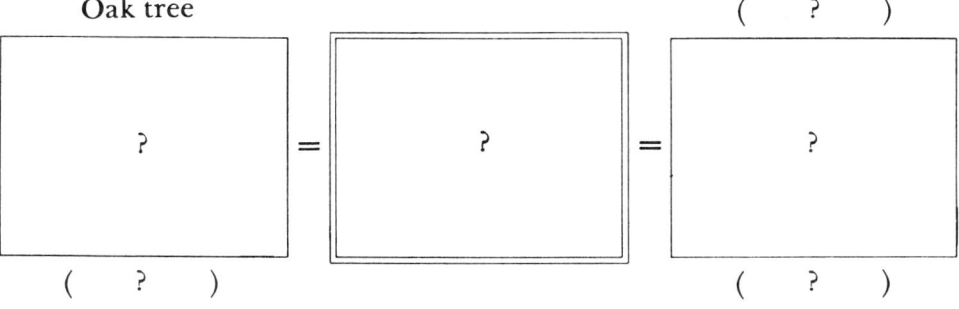

29. What ideas can you derive from this analogy sequence? Can you set up an analogy sequence of your own?

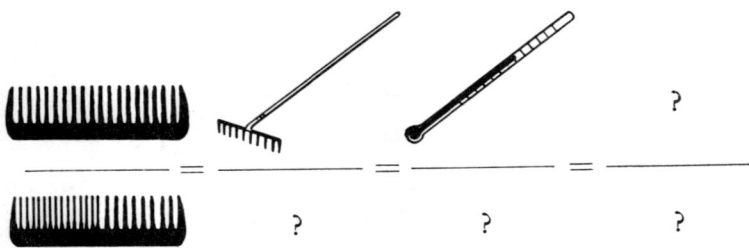

30. By taking the words *hat, feather, red, yellow, blue* and mixing them up in your mind, you may arrive at a new combination, such as "blue feather in yellow hat" — something which may not now exist, in your experience. Can you list several possible qualities of a fountain pen, "mix them up," and thus invent a new type of fountain pen? What other objects or "situations" might you create by listing and manipulating qualities?

31. Which item (a, b, c, or d) is the same as the first?

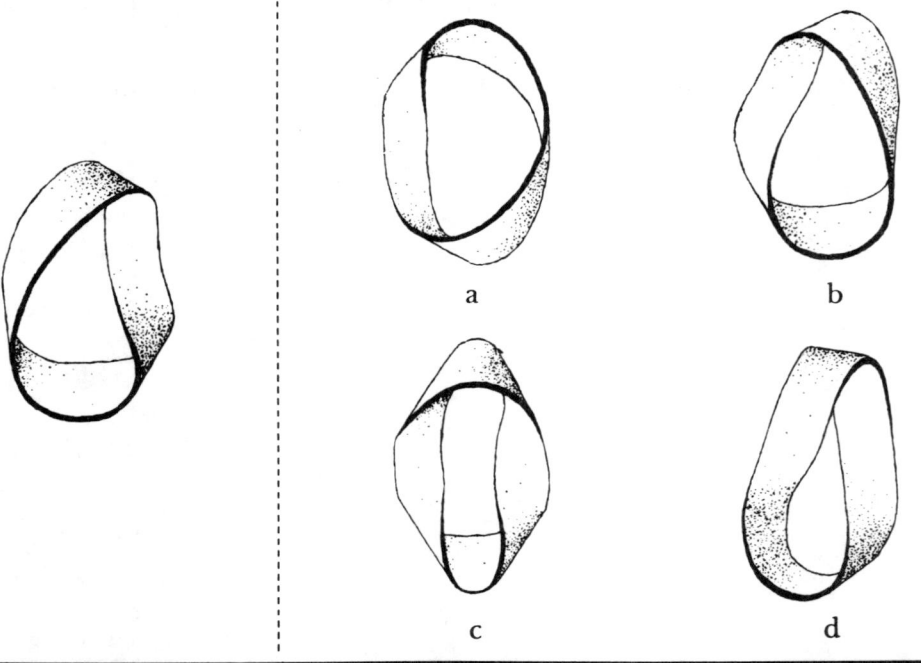

32. Match each use of the word *face* with the corresponding meaning, at right.

She made a *face*.	A	a		Front surface of a person's head.
"And the Spirit of God moved upon the *face* of the waters." *Genesis*	B	b		A grimace; an expressive facial distortion.
Face me when you speak!	C	c		Countenance; expression of emotion.
"Bowed by the weight of centuries he leans Upon his hoe and gazes on the ground, The emptiness of ages in his *face* . . ." Edwin Markham, *The Man with the Hoe*	D	d		Symbolic or marked surface, as of a clock or playing card.
Challenges never evaporate; they must be *faced*.	E	e		A thing's prominent surface, whether upper, front or outer.
Turning the card's *face* up, he revealed a queen.	F	f		To confront a situation with courage and fortitude.
"I have heard of your paintings too, well enough. God hath given you one *face*, and you make yourselves another." William Shakespeare, *Hamlet*	G	g		To be positioned with the face toward someone or something.

33. Was the "man" that God created a structure or an operation?

34. Can you invent a new type of paper clip? One way to start is to list several possible qualities. For example: SUBSTANCE, METAL, PLASTIC, SHAPE, COLOR. . . . By thinking of possible attributes, you can "assemble" in your mind an object which may never before have existed. Remember that qualities may be sensory, emotional, or logical.

35. How does the meaning of *bowl* shift, from the first sentence to the second?   His toe crossed the line as he *bowled*.
He *bowled* a good game.

(a) by qualification (quality to thing), (b) by operation analysis (stage to operation), (c) by analogy

36. In *Hamlet*, Shakespeare describes death as an "undiscovered country from whose bourne [or boundary] no traveler returns." Write another metaphor expressing the idea that once a man dies, he can never resume his former mortal existence.

37. Which sentence (a, b, or c) belongs with the two drawings at left? Why?

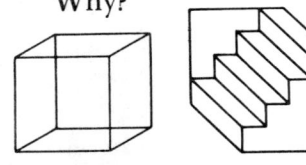

a. No man hath seen God at any time.

b. The Lord is my shepherd.

c. In the beginning, God created the heaven and the earth.

38. Make use of an outline (showing stages and sub-stages) in planning some operation, such as a speech, party, trip, business activity, etc.

39. One of the best ways to generate ideas on any subject is to make a classification diagram. How many sources of power (gasoline, electricity, wind-power, etc.) can you name? Continue the diagram which has been started below.

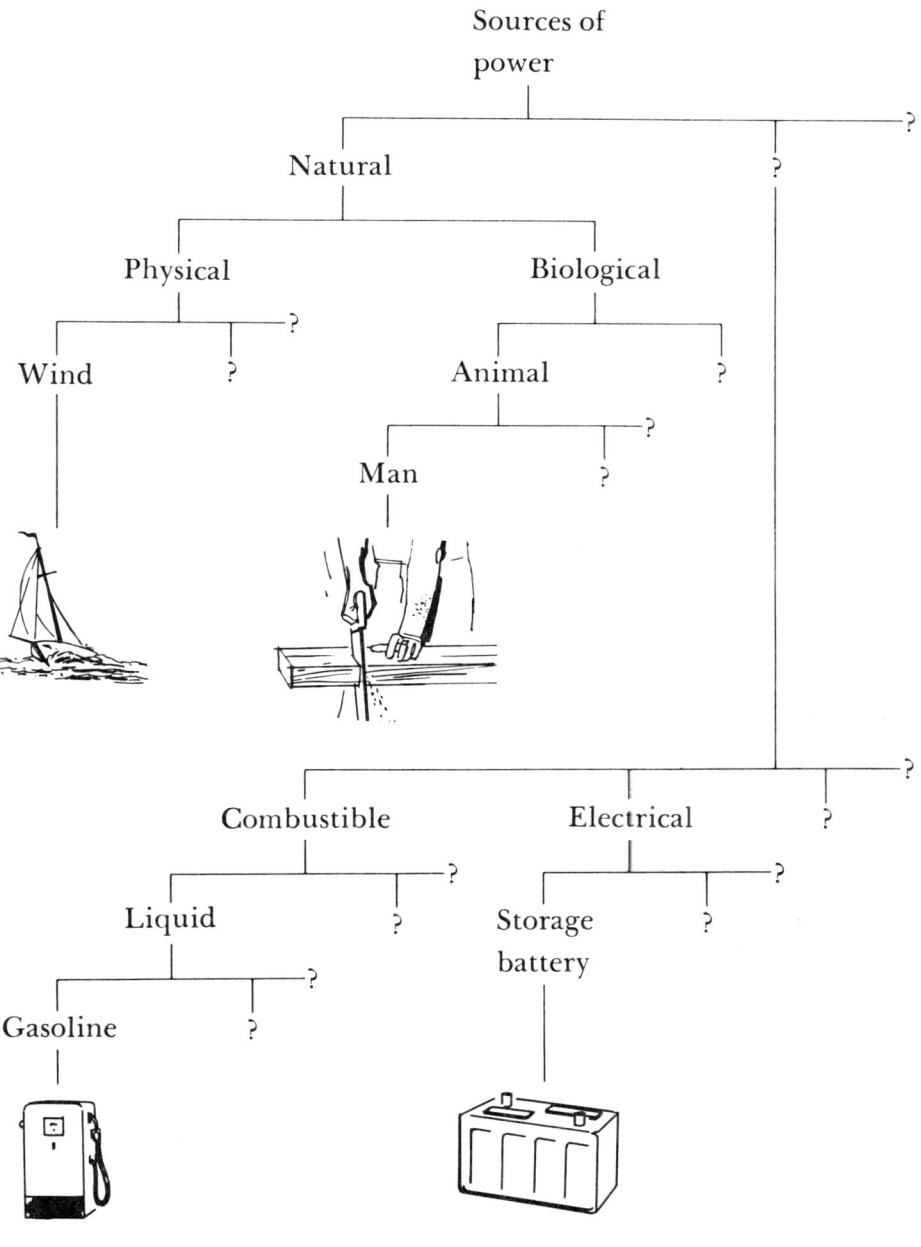

ANSWERS TO EXERCISES

Several of the problems may have more than one "correct" answer. Multiple answers have been listed in some instances, but other equally correct possibilities may have been overlooked. Problems of this sort are really guessing games in which the reader tries to find out what the person who made them up had in mind. If he gets a different answer he is not necessarily wrong, unless there is an inconsistency in his reasoning. Getting a particular answer is less important than the creative mental exercise of considering various possibilities.

LEVEL 1

1. b. Opposite in darkness.
2. a. All are apples.
3. c.
4. b. Hat goes on head as glove fits around right hand; both cover something.
5. c.
6. c. All are circles.
7. a. The word *sweet* names a taste quality of a candy cane as the word *sour* names a taste quality of a lemon.
8. c. Opposite in sex.
9. c. The boy and girl alternate.
10. a. The pattern OXX repeats itself.
11. c. A branch projects from the trunk of a tree as an arm projects from the body of a man.
12. b.
13. A⟶a / B⟶b (crossed)
14. b. It is a square, like the two at left.
15. b. Opposite in orientation (up — down).
16. 5. Each number is two less than the one to its left.
17. d.
18. a. All three are happy, smiling.
19. c. Two lower-case letters follow two upper-case letters for each letter from A through C.
20. b. Opposite in habitat (water — air). Or d. Opposite in "freedom" (free — caught).
21. d.
22. b.
23. b. A football is played with in a football game as a baseball is played with in a baseball game.
24. a. From left to right, the words stand for greater and greater periods of time.
25. b. Opposite in time (beginning — end). Or c. Opposite in type of meaning (process — thing).
26. c. A painter paints a picture as a carpenter builds a house; both create something.
27. c. It is a bird, like the two at left.
28. A⟶a / B⟶b (crossed)

LEVEL 2

1. b.
2. a. Opposite in color signified; red and green are complimentary colors.
3. b. All three are vehicles which float on water.
4. c. Tire makes driving easier for car as shoe makes walking easier for man; both make tractional contact with a surface.
5. b. The series "121212ABABAB" repeats itself.
6. b. It is a spherical object, like the two at left.
7. Consult a dictionary to check your answers.
8. b.
9. c. Petal is a part of a flower as Texas is a part of the United States.
10. c. Opposite in sex and emotion (girl crying — boy smiling).
    Or b. Opposite in hair style (short — long).
11. Round, revolving, alive, symbolic, two-legged, etc.
12. c. Bird is biological counterpart of airplane as fish is biological counterpart of submarine.
13. d. Left hand.
14. A——a
    B——b
15. a. As in the number sequence, the letter sequence should increase from the first value to the fifth value, then decrease the first value.
16. b. A ring for the finger and the disk surrounding Saturn have a similar appearance.
17. a. All three are flying organisms.
18. a. Opposite in age.
19. c.
20. b. All three are types of fruit.
21. b. The sequence "XOXOXXOX-XO" repeats itself.
22. c. Spider traps and devours fly as cat catches and eats mouse; both capture and devour a prey.
23. The word THE upside-down. This exercise illustrates the principle of "thing-making"; the objects that we experience are "made" in our minds.
24. b/f   c   e   a/d.
25. c. It is a type of food, like the two at left.
    Or b. It is a "fruit" of nature, not manufactured.
26. b. Child will grow into old man as morning will progress into evening; both will change or be transformed into a later stage of a "happening."
27. b. Opposite in emotion signified.
    Or a. Opposite in initial letter (consonant — vowel).
28. A⤫a
    B⤫b
29. Knife { Blade ____ Handle ____ }
30. a. Opposite in "openness" (closed — open).
31. b. The last two lines should rhyme, as do the first two; the last line should have four syllables, like the second line, since the first and third lines have the same number of syllables.
32. c. All three are flowers or blossoms.
33. No "right" answer.
34. Rover.
35. "Grows in" or "Is laid by" or?
36. b. Opposite in utility (hammer acts upon nail, its "object").
    Or d. Opposite in size and power.
37. A⤫a
    B⤫b
    C⤫c

LEVEL 3

1. b. All three have five main veins.
2. a. Opposite in signification of degree of "correspondence" (extremely different — extremely similar).
3. b. The sequence "ABACA" repeats itself.
4. b. Sharp-sounding name is to spiked drawing as smooth-sounding name is to flowing drawing.
5. d.
6. Consult a dictionary to check your answers.
7. a. Moon orbits Earth as Earth orbits Sun.
8. a. Opposite in either reality or mortality, according to your belief (mythical — real, or immortal — mortal).
9.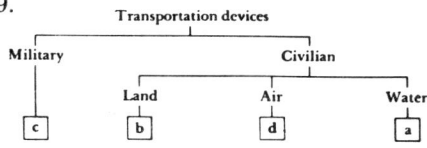
10. "Flys in," "Swims in," or?
11. 150 pounds.
12. b. The eye opens, goes from center to left to right to center, then closes.
13. b. It has a spiral pattern, like the two objects at left.
14. c. All three are striking or hitting implements.
    Or a. All are made of metal.
15. Does it look like a woman to you? Recall John Donne's poem, "Go and catch a falling star / Get with child a mandrake root..."
16. Consult a dictionary to check your answers.
17. c.
18. a. The numbers increase according to the pattern "plus one, plus two, plus three," which repeats itself.
19. Sex, male, female, living, emotion, happy, hair style, etc. Notice that sorting factors may be of two types: naming differences (e. g. sex) or naming similarities (e. g. male).
20. b. The hen is a female, like the woman and the cow.
    Or c. All are mammals.
21.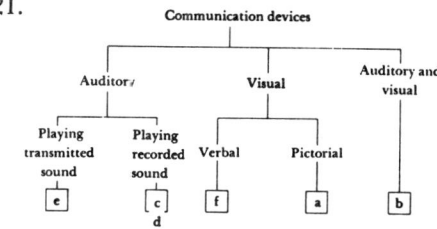
22. a. Opposite in case (upper case — lower case).
23. a. In both cases the same picture is turned upside-down.
24. b. Cold-blooded, vertebrate sea creatures are a species (sub-class) of the genus (including class) which contains all animal life. Note that in taxonomy *genus* and *species* have different meanings than those which appear here.
25. b. The small black circle advances a single space each time; the white circle alternately advances two spaces and one space; the large black circle advances two spaces each time; each circle reverses its motion when the semicircular base has been traversed.
26. A———a
    B———b (crossed)
27. c. All three are forms of animal life.
28. Did you divide the people into HAPPY, CRYING, and SURPRISED; and then each group into MALE and FEMALE?
29. "Is propelled by" or?
30. b. Opposite in mood (sour — happily carefree).
31.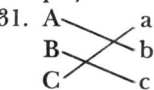
32. b. The "ocean" is a whole, includ-

ing as parts several "oceans": the Pacific, Atlantic, Indian, Arctic, and Antarctic.
33. c. Undivided circles are divided into white and black as undivided squares are divided into white and black.
34. b.
35. Changing circle
    Changing in size
        Growing smaller
        Growing larger
    Changing in shade
        Growing lighter
        Growing darker
36. Sorting circles
    Sorting by color
    Sorting by size
        Sorting blacks into large, medium, and small
        Sorting whites into large, medium and small
37. b. All three are pliable objects (also, capable of emitting fluid).
38. You might have sorted circles by color and then by size, or by size and then by color.
39. No "right" answer. Does your answer create an analogy in your mind?
40. c. Birth is the beginning point of life as sunrise is the beginning point of a day.
41. a. All three are "balanced" objects; the two parts of each are identical.
42. No "right" answer. Exercises of this type can help you to think up analogies and to write metaphors.
43. a. A vegetable mushroom and the cloud of an atomic blast have a similar appearance.
44. c. An electron is an outer, orbiting part of an atom as a planet is an outer, orbiting part of a solar system.
45. No "right" answer.
46.

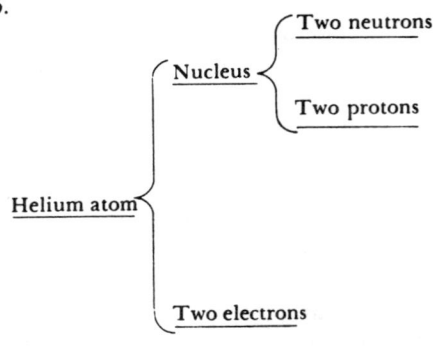

47. No "right" answer.

LEVEL 4

1. c. Opposite in dimension of measurement (time — space).
2. b. All three words can signify a visual quality, a type of impression perceived with the eyes.
3. b. Opposite in brightness (bright — dark).
4. Consult a dictionary to check your answers.
5. a. Rent is assessed by the month as gasoline is sold by the gallon.
6. b. All three are acts of cooperation or "communication."
7. c. Two small circles make a large one of the same color; large black and large white circles appear alternately.
8. d. Upside down.
9. Season, winter, summer, team, individual, competitive, bodily contact, place, land, water, air, etc.
10. Is pounded into wood by   Is inserted into wood by
11. b. From left to right, the numbers increase by one; from top to bottom, they increase by two.
12. A a
    B b
    C———c

13. Consult a dictionary to check your answers.
14. d. Opposite in symmetry (symmetrical — asymmetrical).
15. b. All three are fronts or "faces." Or c. All three run mechanically.
16. This exercise illustrates that the perception of "things" involves the mental imposition of pattern upon raw sensations.
17. d. The words become progressively more inclusive.
18. a. All three are measuring instruments.
    Or c. All three are oblong and about the same length.
19.

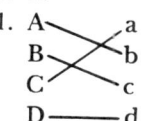

20. writes   creates   paints
21. Nancy, if proximity is the only consideration; otherwise Mary, who is by far the prettier.
22. b.
23. c. Opposite in "level of representation" (picture of a real man — picture of a picture of a real man).
24.

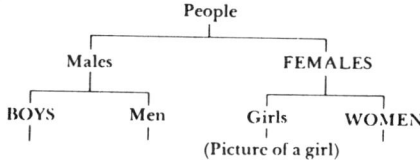

25. No "right" answer. Recall that a metaphor (if "proportional") is a type of analogy.
26. c.
27. The question is, of course, ambiguous, and can have no precise meaning until all its terms are defined. You might benefit from looking up the word *word* in a dictionary.
28. d. Opposite in function (is directed —directs).
    Or a., opposite in mobility
29. b. All three are organisms, or living things.
30. d.
31.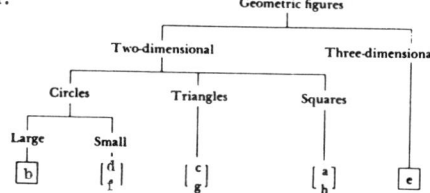
32. a and d
33. No "right" answer. You should have created a classification of your own, thinking up sorting factors, genera, species, and specimens (ways).
34. No "right" answer. What analogy does your answer embody?
35. A—a
    B—b
    C——c
36. Solving formula
    A. Preparing for computations
        1. Writing formula
        2. Listing values of symbols
        3. Substituting values for symbols in formula
    B. Solving formula
        1. Computations within parentheses
            A. Computations above line
                1. Dividing 18 by 2
                2. Subtracting 3 from 9
            B. Dividing 6 by 2
        2. Computations outside of parentheses
            (Adding 3 and 12)
37. b. Earth orbits the Sun as Hungary is politically and economically controlled by Russia; both are "satellites" of something.
38. A dinosaur? A sea horse? Or? This is an exercise in thing-making.
39. No "Right" answer.
    Choices a, b, and c can each be rationalized.
40. a. All three are natural objects (as opposed to manufactured).
41. Consult a dictionary to check your answers.
42. c. Opposite in dimension (two-di-

mensional — three-dimensional).
43. a. Opposite in direction symbolized (south — north).
    Or b. Opposite in type of letter (consonant — vowel).
44. No "right" answer.
45. Did you divide it into top and bottom, and then the bottom into left and right?
46. $10.00. Did you make a classification diagram? The problem is difficult to solve without one, or *some* method of classifying the data.
47. Any solution is proper, so long as it is consistent. Possibly the most difficult aspect of classification is choosin which sorting factors to use.
48. This exercise illustrates a structural verbal shift.
49. c. Circles are divided into white and black as people are divided into dark-haired and blond.
50. b.
51. You might have divided the series by letter within case (lower and upper).
52. A — a
    B ✗ b
    C ✗ c
    D — d
53. c. Red is to green (spelled backwards) as a girl is to an upside-down boy; both are different from something in two ways.
54. c. A "helix" is a quality (spiral shape) which is found in a helix (a type of mollusk).
55. a. All three are figures which have their own shapes repeated inside.
56. No "right" answer.

LEVEL 5

1. b. There are two overlapping series: "12345" and "54321"; the X's are superfluous.
2. c. In the sea, a cold-blooded fish is to a warm-blooded fish as, on land, a cold blooded animal is to a warm-blooded animal.
3. Consult a dictionary to check your answers.
4. The words *largest* and *smallest* are, of course, ambiguous; this exercise illustrates that terms must be defined before a problem can be solved.
5. c. The "planets" travel around the "sun" at various rates; the "moon" travels around the middle "planet."
6. Consult a dictionary to check your answers.
7. L (number)
   E (happy)
   S (bright)
   L (increasing, or becoming filled)
   E (sad or dejected)
   S (sound)
8. c. All three are symmetrical objects.
9. c. Opposite in level of generalization (species — genus).
    Or d. Opposite in "purity" (primary — secondary).
10. b. Opposite in "meaning contrast" (antonyms — synonyms).
11. c. All three are one of a pair.
12. c. *Coin* is a genus term for *dime* as *bill* is a genus term for *dollar*.
13. Consult a dictionary to check your answers.
14. Humility.
15. b. Opposite in "side" (back — front).
16. A — a
    B ✗ b
    C — c
17. Shape.
    Size.
    Color is ignored.
18. No "right" answer.
19. No "right" answer.
20. A — a
    B ✗ b
    C ✗ c
    D — d
21. b. Circles are divided into large and

small as people are divided into tall and short.
22. a. All three are "recipients" of something which travels through the air (an arrow, focused light, a baseball).
23. No "right" answer. Which mental process did you follow in making up the new sense: thing-making, qualification, classification, structure analysis, operation analysis, analogy, or a combination of these?
24. No "right" answer. You may divide any operation into whatever stages and sub-stages you wish, according to your purpose.
25. c. These words are ambiguous and can be used in many different senses; when these senses correspond, the words are synonyms (as, the French *state* and the English *nation*).
26. Did you mentally divide the structure into parts?
27.

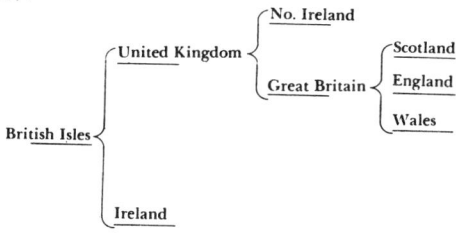

28. b.
29. No "right" answer.
30. No "right" answer.
31. c. All three measure spatial dimensions (as opposed to temporal).
32. a.
33.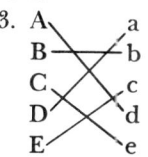
34. A   D   F
    B
    C
    E
35. No "right" answer.
36. b. One side of the scales weighs the same as the other side as one "side" of an account equals the other "side"; A is related to B as C is related to D.
37. No "right" answer. Any solution is satisfactory, so long as you divided the happening into main and sub-stages.
38. b. The moving figures are black when in the top half of the square, white when in the bottom half. The circle moves counter-clockwise two spaces at a time, alternating between large and small. The square and the triangle move clockwise a space at a time.
39. c.
40. If you did not classify the words, you probably did not remember very many of them.
41. No "right" answer.

LEVEL 6

1. d. The series "XOXOXOXXOX-OOXOXOXXXOXOXOXX" repeats itself.
2. b. Opposite in degree of circular movement (going around in a circle — moving back and forth in an arc).
3. Any analysis is satisfactory, so long as you divided the structure into parts and sub-parts.
4. Consult a dictionary to check your answers.
5. b. Stylized pyramid is to real pyramid as stylized heart is to real heart.
6. b. A single pull of the arm through the water is a stage of a "stroke," which includes many arm movements, together with movements of the legs.
7. No "right" answer.
8. There is no "correct" answer, of course; this exercise simply illustrates that before any problem can

be solved, careful definition of terms must take place; how should the word *square* be defined?
9. c. All three are ambiguous (or reversable) figures. (So are a and b, though less obviously so.)
10.   Worry
      Money
11. a.
12. missing.
13. a. Each of the three items is the beginning of a sequence (life, the alphabet, numbering — 1, 2, 3).
14. d. Opposite in order of spatial inclusion (sub-part to whole — whole to sub-part).
15. b. An hour is a "time part" of a day as horses are a type of animal.
16. No "right" answer.
17. a.
18. c. The female parent of a human being is a species of the genus which includes the female parents of all animals.
19. b. Identical circles are sorts of circles of many sizes as identical girls are sorts of a wider category of people.
20. No "right" answer.
21. No "right" answer.
22. c. All three are parts of a total system, unable to function by themselves.
23.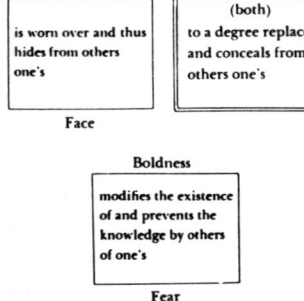
24. No. But the word *squeak*, meaning the cry of a mouse, might grow to mean the similar sound of new shoes.
25. c. The dots are expanding while revolving.
26. No "right" answer.
27. a.
28. Did you divide day into daytime and night and daytime into constituent stages?
29. d. Opposite in type of opposition ("fit" or "displacement" opposition — mirror-image opposition).
30. If you did not think of parts within parts, you probably were not able to sketch the figure.
31. Consult a dictionary to check your answers.
32. c. The contents of all three circles indicate general classes.
33.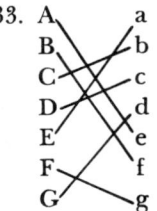
34. No "right" answer.
35. No "right" answer.
36. No "right" answer.
37. No "right" answer.
38. d. The numbers follow the repetitive pattern of "plus three, minus one, minus one"; the letters go through the alphabet sequentially, alternating capital and lower case; also, the *number* of numbers in each group decreases by one, as the number of letters in each group increases by one.
39. No "right" answer.
40. No "right" answer.

LEVEL 7

1. c. Opposite in type of sorting factor (color — size).
2. Consult a dictionary to check your answers.

3. a. Opposite in degree of signified generality (proper name — generalization).
4. c. A church building is a part of the larger "church" which includes the minister and the congregation. Operational considerations may also play a role in this verbal shift, to the extent that church *functions* are taken into account.
5. a. All three are symbols, as opposed to observable things.
6. Consult a dictionary to check your answers.
7. Did you divide the sequence into segments?
8. b. All three are ambiguous drawings. Is the sun rising or setting? Or c. All three involve "twoness."
9. c. Circles are a type of geometric figures as cats are a type of animals.
10. No "right" answer.
11. No "right" answer.
12. d.
13. Actually, the map itself is already an analyzed structure. A structure analysis diagram is simply a diagrammatic translation.
14. a. Opposite in order of inclusion (all-inclusive to particular — particular to all-inclusive).
15. SET, which has over two hundred recorded senses. Be careful! The word *ambiguous* is ambiguous, too; you might look it up in a dictionary.
16. Did you define the word or the thing? If you defined the word, did you define it in one sense or in multiple senses? You should have thought of several possible meanings of the word. If you did not, perhaps you should look it up in a dictionary.
17. No "right" answer.
18. c. All three are forms of classification (as opposed to structure analysis or operation analysis).
19. 5,783. Did you divide the dots into parts (areas, clusters, constellations, etc.)?
20. b. A tooth is a part of a gear as a baseball is a part of a baseball game.
21. No "right" answer.
22. c.
23. On a planet which revolves in ten hours; of course, *day* shifts in meaning.
24.

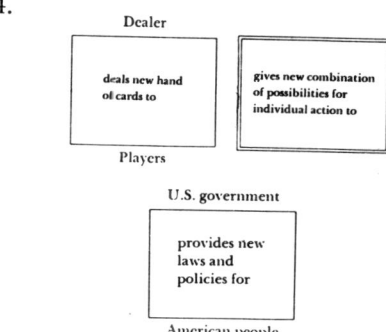

25. No "right" answer.
26. No "right" answer.
27. No "right" answer.
28.

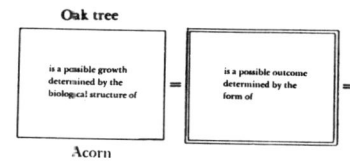

29. No "right" answer.
30. No "right" answer.
31. a.
32.

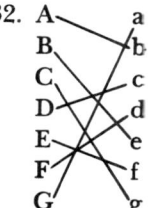

33. No "right" answer.
34. No "right" answer.

35. b. A single pitch of the ball is a stage of the total operation of a game of bowling.
36. No "right" answer.
37. b. It is a metaphor; like the figures at left, it has two meanings in one stimulus.
38. No "right" answer.
39. No "right" answer.